Called By Grace

To Glory

Diane Hallenbeck

ACKNOWLEDGMENTS

God calls us out of darkness and into His marvelous light and He uses amazing people in that process. My husband Kevin has loved and nurtured me all these years and I thank God for such a fabulous traveling companion on this road Home. I want to acknowledge Dr. Dan Williams for his role in leading me to Christ and to a place of being able to hear God's voice of love and to Cindy, his wife, for loving me and editing this study and living life together, even though far apart. I am honored to be their "daughter." Many thanks, as well, to Kathi Fournier and Anna Wallich for pouring over this manuscript.

To the Women of Bethany Covenant and the Sweet Tuesdays Bible Study, thank you for helping me grow and for encouraging me to write this book. To my family and friends, thanks for the love and encouragement you have given. May God lead you on this fabulous journey by His grace. May you be His glorious child!

INTRODUCTION

God has placed this amazing call on our lives to be changed by His word. Sometimes we limit the power of what God can do by what we believe about Him or ourselves or others. I wrote this study to challenge the ways we have always thought about ourselves and God. I enjoy reading Early Church Fathers' writings because, while complex, often their words do not contain our twenty-first century jargon, and I find I can hear truth very clearly. It also serves to remind me that our perceptions and feelings are not unique to our century, but span the ages.

So, listen. God is speaking. God's word has the power to change us, no matter who we are or how we have lived. I invite you on a journey to look into His word, examine it for yourself and listen for God's voice of love calling you. May God's grace flood you and His Holy Spirit lead you as you journey by grace to glory.

CONTENTS

Chapter 1

Called To Mourn

"My heart is stirred by a noble theme as I recite my verses for the King; my tongue is the pen of a skillful writer. You are the most excellent of men and your lips have been anointed with grace since God has blessed you forever. Gird your sword upon your side, O mighty One; clothe yourself with splendor and majesty" (Psalm 45:1-3).

David pens a beautiful Psalm, entitled, "The King and His beauty." I would like us to approach this Psalm with a heart that asks questions about our King and our relationship to Him. I want the words of David to frame a journey to the heart of God. I trust this Psalm will show us God's true character and His heart of love for us. God's Word holds so many treasures for us: "dig deep" and find for yourself new ways of seeing God, yourself and perhaps others as well.

Turn with me and take a close look at David's words: "In your majesty ride forth victoriously in behalf of truth, humility and righteousness; let your right hand display awesome deeds. Let your sharp arrows pierce the hearts of the King's enemies; let the nations fall beneath your feet" (Psalm 45:4, 5). Here we have the Lord establishing His authority, power and ability to rule and reign in a righteous Kingdom. There is no question that

His heart is good: "ride forth on behalf of truth, humility and righteousness…you love righteousness and hate wickedness" (verses 4, 7). First and foremost in our minds we need to consider that the King who calls us is good. "Taste and see that the Lord is good," writes David in Psalm 34:8. Before we can consider the call of God on our hearts and lives we to look at our view of Him very carefully.

Read 1 Peter 2:3-5

1. Do we believe God is good?

Peter assumes our experience of God is one of goodness. The call of Peter is the same one the psalmist gives. The call in or of our lives is to live for God, to be in His house, building up His house with our very lives. First, though, we must examine ourselves and see what we believe. If you had to define "good" what would you say? Webster's Dictionary offers an amazing assortment of definitions for us.

To be "good" is to be: of a favorable character or tendency; bountiful; handsome, attractive; suitable fit; free from injury or disease; whole; certain to last; agreeable, pleasant; deserving of respect; virtuous, just, commendable; of the highest worth or reliability.

Do I view God this way? Have I looked at my faith and my perception of God and included any of these definitions? The real issue for me is that *sometimes* I view God favorably, but only when He does the things I ask for or answers my prayers the way I want. Otherwise I view Him as unfair or not reliable and then I am in trouble. If my view of God changes with my circumstances I need to acknowledge this as wrong. God does not change. My situation, my feelings, my perceptions of God, and my "demands" on God - all these change, but God never changes. His heart towards me is one of a Father to a child, one of a bridegroom to a bride. I am "His beloved," as the author Henri Nouwen would say. The sooner I cement this into my heart the more I will begin to trust Him. If I believe the lie that "God doesn't care about me," then I have made God into a "mean God" who hurts me. I have to be honest; this is very personal and difficult "stuff" to look at in ourselves, much less share with anyone. Yet God is waiting. He does not want us to worship Him with our lips but have our hearts far from Him (see Isaiah 29:13). Be sure that your heart is as near to God as your words say you are. This is what matters to God. He is good and He wants us to know Him. To know Him is to know Him as good.

Read Psalm 117: 1, 2; 1 Corinthians 1:9

2. How have we experienced God in our lives?

Have we experienced Him as faithful? Have we known Him to be good to us and our families? Have we experienced Him as kind and loving? All of our own personal history becomes the magnifying glass we put God under. We might say to Him, "You let this happen in my life, and so I do not trust you to be good." Or, "You didn't give me this in my life, or that - a child, a healing, a job, a sensitive husband, and now I don't trust you to be good." You see, God has not changed. Other times in our lives might be filled with praise and wonder for all God has done: "Thank you God, for this job or that move." "Thank you God for this child or that teacher." The magnifying glass we hold then scrutinizes God and finds He is good, and so we praise Him. Truly, "God is good." It is just that we perceive Him through our pain one way and then through our joy another. Our magnifying glass changes with our experience, but over and over in the Bible, God tells us He never changes (see Hebrews 13:8).

Have we, "now that we have grown up in our salvation, tasted and seen that the Lord is good?" (1 Peter 2:3) This question is crucial to our faith, because underneath all our experiences in this life we need to have the bedrock faith of this: "No one is good, except God alone" (Luke 18:19). Our experiences in life do not always leave us assured of God's goodness. If we have suffered or those we love have suffered, we find ourselves questioning the goodness of God. But in scripture, God declares His goodness as a fact rather than an experience. He tells us that He is good. What we experience in our lives may not always be good, but one thing is sure. God is good. This is something one must take by faith that not all of our life experience will line up on the side of "God is good." If we have suffered abuse as a child, or have had teenagers disappoint us, or family members suffer from cancer then we will say, "How can God be good?" If our life lacks meaning or direction and we wonder what purpose we have then we may ask, "How can God be good?" We are tempted to pick up our magnifying glass and view our world and God through the eyes of pain and disappointment and our conclusion, faulty as our perceptions of God may be, is that God is not good and cannot be trusted. This is our pain speaking, our deep hurt: our own soul has been wounded and we find we do not know how to trust God.

I have a favorite Early Church Father, a Bishop who was writing in the fourth century. He spent most of his life as a Pastor and wrote extensively on how to interpret the Bible. His name is John Chrysostom, and he writes this about our wounds:

> "Come now, let me relieve the wound of your despondency, and disperse the thoughts which gather this cloud of care around you. For what is it which upsets your mind and why are you sorrowful and dejected…we can trust the Pilot in all this- not one who gets the better of the storm by his art, but calms the raging waters by His rod."[1]

There is a wound we receive when we are despondent. It is like an arrow that pierces our soul and tells us, so subtly, "God isn't really good." Well, at least that is my wound. Over and over again in my life when I have suffered, I would find my heart saying, "God doesn't really care about me." But you see, this wound can be relieved and even cured. As Chrysostom points out earlier, "But let us know ourselves. Let us know our wounds. For thus we shall be able to apply the medicines. For he who does not know his disease, will give no care to his weakness."[2]

The medicine my heart needs is truth: God is good. This is the frame of reference for our whole lives. Nothing else makes sense really. To believe God is good is to allow God to comfort us when our life doesn't make sense, when our hearts are broken with grief. We can no more be comforted by God than we can open a locked door without a key, unless we believe God is good. This is the key to being comforted by God, the key to being embraced and enfolded by His love. Once we have settled in our hearts, for certain and for sure, that God is good, then our hearts are opened to receive His goodness and comfort in our sorrows and disappointments.

Read Psalm 45:10, 11; Deuteronomy 21:10-14

3. What are we asked to do after we are listening?

We have a good King who apparently desires us; but before we can truly embrace the King's call to know Him and have Him know us we have significant emotional work to do. The call in Psalm 45 is a call to mourn: "Forget your people and your father's house." This is mourning. The obscure little passage in Deuteronomy 21 sheds some amazing light on this call to mourn. A foreign woman has come into her captor's house and how does she feel? Frightened, scared, alone, and sad, and now she has been approached to become this captor's wife! Her mourning, her change of clothes, signifies a "putting off" of her old life and embracing a new life. This call is for us as well as we come into God's house. We too must forget. We must forget our old ways of life, our old habits, and our family traditions if they weren't ones that honor God. There is so much to forget when you have come from a place of captivity, from a place where you have not known God and now you do. Does this woman know God as "good?" Perhaps not, as she is a captive in an Israelite home, but God has provided for her. First He gives her time to grieve, and then He gives her honor as the man must marry her and may not keep her as a slave. She is bestowed the honor of a wife. She has much to grieve, yes, her home, her family, her traditions, her hopes and dreams, but then God seems to be providing a new home, a new family, new traditions, new hopes and dreams. Is this very unlike what God does for us?

First of all there is a process we go through as we are called by God's grace to enter God's House. The first is surely to "believe on the Lord Jesus Christ and you shall be saved" (Acts 16:31a). God calls us into His house by faith and we truly become His. We believe that He has come to save us and then we "give up" or get rid of all those things in our lives that do not honor God. Maybe we grieve family relationships, maybe we give up traditions and dreams and hopes that don't really honor God. Many things need to be "forgotten" on that narrow road Jesus talks about. Maybe we have hurts and wounds that are so deep we feel we can never mourn them, and never let go of them. Jesus speaks to that. Have you heard His words? "A bruised reed He will not break and a dimly burning wick He will not quench" (Isaiah 42:3). Begin the process. Allow God into those places in your heart where you are wounded or may have been wounded. Sit in His healing presence and just grieve. Take all your expectations, your demands, and your hurts and allow

Him access to your heart. You may be surprised at His heart of love and His tender compassion.

Read Isaiah 61:1- 3

4. Do you believe that Jesus came to rescue you, save you, bind up your hurts, and comfort you?

The promises of Isaiah are staggering. Christ has come to do an amazing inner work -to bind up broken hearts and free us from beliefs, memories and experiences that hold us captive. Is your heart broken over a relationship: your marriage, your children, or a friendship that has soured? Can you see that Christ came for those very things? He has come to touch our hearts and bring hope and healing, to bring gladness again. He has come to bring us from the place of a captive in His house mourning, to the place where we are His beloved. Isaiah 61 is a call to a changed life, to a free life. It is a chance to be authentic with God; actually bringing our wounds and hurts to Him to be made whole instead of covering them over. He wants to meet us in our brokenness and bring us to a place of abundant life. The abundance is inner -joy for sorrow, the garment of praise for a spirit of heaviness. These are not just words on a page. This is the living active Word of God! God wants to comfort us while we mourn and provide for us while we grieve. Do the inner work with the grace of God and allow yourself to become "a planting of the Lord, for the display of His splendor!" (Isaiah 63:1)

Read John 8:31-36

5. Do you need freedom from something?

Here again we find that the Lord has come to set us free. We may feel we need freedom from some kind of compulsive behavior - perhaps eating or shopping (my husband would be thrilled if I was "set free" from this behavior!) There can be deep emotional reasons for the behaviors we find ourselves almost unable to control. I know that God can "set us free," but often times if things are deep-seated then we will need the help of good friends or professional counselors who are trained to help us understand the "why" of our behaviors. Ask God to provide those friends or those counselors that He will use in your life to help "set you free." Christ has come to set us free from something so deep-seated that we are often unaware of it in our lives: sin. We may be living a very pleasant life, have a wonderful family, good friends, no apparent addictions/dysfunctions/obsessions and we feel really great about ourselves, but there is one problem: we have not faced our own true nature. Just as the Jews in John 8 could not see they were slaves to sin, so it is in our lives as well. Each of us has fallen short of God's holiness. We can look out into the heavens on a clear fall day and marvel at the beauty of the sky, the birds, the changing leaves and we just know: Someone greater than us has made this whole magnificent world. He is good and He is holy.

Read Romans 1:18-20; Colossians 1:15, 16

6. What do we need an excuse from?

We need an excuse for not recognizing God for who He is and for not recognizing our own sin, self-centeredness, pride, our ideas that get in the way of God speaking to us and working in our lives, our selfishness, our constant need for attention or approval or life to be the way we want it to be. All of these can be called sin - sin is "missing the mark" of the perfect life that God calls us to - of loving Him and others and ourselves in a way that reflects His glory and perfection. Of course, on this side of heaven we can never reach this kind of love and perfection, but we are called to it: "Be perfect, therefore, as your heavenly Father is perfect" (Matthew 5:48). So, what have we to be set free from? Almost every day I need to be set free from myself! From my sin! I need to be freed from my own pride and selfishness, from choosing my own way rather than God's way. We need to recognize ourselves as captives to sin and truly God's enemies. Romans 5:10 spells it out in very stark terms: we were God's enemies and now we are reconciled to God by the death of His Son Jesus Christ. "How much more shall we be saved through His life?" (verse 10) Picture "Prince Charming" here. Picture yourself far from God and behind enemy lines; you aren't even sure you would have chosen to be on the enemies' side, but there you are because of your own sin, other's sin and the separation that is a reality when we try to approach God while we are "still in our sin" (Romans 5:8). Keep using your imagination and picture yourself on the side of sin and separated from God. Jesus comes to "set the captives free" (Isaiah 61:1). He is carrying us on the back of His white horse, riding with us out of darkness and danger and into His Kingdom of love. That is how I picture Colossians 1:13 -- the great rescue.

Let us apply the light of these scriptures. We were, at one time, prisoners of the dominion of darkness - literally enemies of God because we were separated from God by sin. Then, God rescued us; He captured the captives and placed us in His house. God has gone to war against His enemies and taken us captive. He places us in His house, in the Kingdom of the Son He loves and then He is enthralled by our beauty. The Old Testament passage is clear: the beautiful woman is to be taken into His home and then she is to mourn shaving her head, trimming her nails (I'm not sure why she is doing that!) and then putting away the clothes she was wearing when she was taken captive. After a period of living in His house in mourning, she may then become His wife.

Read Jeremiah 31:3, 4, 13

7. Have you done this? Have you lived in God's house and mourned?

What do we have to mourn? God has called us and loved us and taken us out of the kingdom of darkness and placed us in His house. But, sometimes we need to mourn the places we have been (or sometimes the place we are right now.) The kingdom of darkness can be frightening and its hold on us very powerful. We need to mourn the things that have happened to us and those we love: sickness, death, losses, broken dreams, miscarriages, abuse, neglect, betrayal, just the heartbreak of the world.

We need to mourn our view of God. Sometimes we have lived in His house for so long and if we do not mourn, a subtle simmering contempt for God fills our hearts. "Why doesn't God do this? Why doesn't God do that? Why doesn't God heal my father, fix my teenagers or change my husband? Why didn't God save my parent's marriage? Why didn't God save my baby or heal my child?" On and on our hearts cry while silently these unanswered questions build a wall of un-mourned losses. Instead of being in God's house mourning, we are in God's house fuming, but, oh, so very politely. We are angry. God gives us the remedy, but we are not sure we want to "take His medicine." The remedy God offers us is mourning. Be angry, yes, but then allow the hurt to melt into tears and grief as we allow God to comfort us. We are in the safest place of all to mourn when we are in God's house. His love and protection surround us and all our pain can find a place of true healing in His house. Remember He has come to "bind up the broken-hearted and comfort all who mourn" (Isaiah 61:2).

Some of us may be wondering what we have to mourn. We have a fantastic faith, a wonderful childhood and we have almost a golden rainbow spreading behind us. Yet even we have disappointments, frustrations, unanswered prayers, and all this needs to be mourned. Others of us look back and see a war-zone; literally devastation and ruins of relationships and heartache at our own choices and others' choices in our lives. Grieve over your sin and the ways you have let God down, grieve over other's sins and the way you feel that God has let you down. Mourn over relationships with parents and spouses. I dare you to be real with God; for once you are real with him, you will realize you have handed Him the key to your heart. All the pain you might have had locked up inside you is now an open door to Him - if you will grieve and mourn and share your pain with God then He is free to come in to your heart and comfort you. Here is the God who comes and "binds up the broken-hearted, proclaims freedom for the captives and release from the darkness, to comfort all who mourn..." (Isaiah 61:1, 2). Did God say He would comfort "some" who mourn? No, He promises to comfort **ALL** who mourn, I am not promising you an easy fix, but I am saying God can handle your pain, your grief, your anger, your emotions. If you will let Him, He will comfort you.

Read Psalm 6:1-9

8. What are you mourning today?

Your sin, another's sin against you, your parent's divorce, your child's rebellion, your spouse's betrayal, (betrayal comes in all forms, doesn't it - there may be an outright affair, or maybe there is neglect, apathy, busyness or even actual abuse in the forms of physical, mental or emotional), all these are deep betrayals that must be mourned. Your bankruptcy, your friend's betrayal, your parent's illness and old age, your view of God giving you a "perfect life" and it not matching up with reality, these, too, need to be mourned.

What is it that is breaking your heart? Ask God, the God who sent His Son to bind up the broken-hearted, to come and bind up your broken heart and comfort you. Mourning our sin and other's sins in our lives, mourning our disappointments and heartaches breaks our heart open and allows God access to our hearts. When we keep a wall of protection around our heart like a "strong fortress" we will be hardened by all that un-grieved agony. The Psalmist in Psalm 18:1, 2 says that God is his fortress, his deliverer and his refuge. We can choose, can we not, to have God as our fortress, running to him for shelter or protection, or we can be running from God, hiding behind our own walls that we think will protect us from hurt. I did this for years. I had a painful childhood, came to know Christ at nineteen, and just thought I could lock a freezer door (it was a BIG freezer) on all that pain and just move on with "being a Christian"- no one told me all the pain and anger and grief would defrost over the course of my life! Just in the last few years have I been able to look at all the puddles of pain that have seeped out of that "freezer of past hurts" and actually allow God to comfort me and heal my heart. Allow God access, let Him take you captive and find you beautiful, let Him call you to mourn so that you might be open to letting go of all the past hurt and be open to all He has for you as His precious possession.

"God, you know our hurts, you know the places we are deeply grieving, places and situations we might not even be able to share. Please, God, come to us. Make us whole. Be our healer, as You have said You would. God, bring us to Your house and help us to mourn that we might become your beautiful bride. In Christ's name we pray, Amen.

Chapter 2

Called to Be Loved

"Now listen, daughter, don't miss a word: forget your country, put your home behind you. Be here- the King is wild for you" (Psalm 45:10, 11; *The Message Translation***).**

How many of us are comfortable with the image of God being "wild" for us? Eugene Peterson uses strong words here in his translation, but they come straight from the heart of God, if you have ears to hear them. The NIV translation is a little milder, it reads: "The King is enthralled by your beauty." What does it mean for God to be wild for us or be enthralled by our beauty? Can we even believe these words are written for us and about us? Before we take a look at the scripture that reveals God's heart towards us, I want to tell you a story.

We got a hound dog a few months ago. His name is Chaplain, and somehow, I have this romantic notion that Chaplain will be some sort of guide to our five children. I keep telling my husband that they need a dog to love them unconditionally because I'm not always able to. I'm not sure how my theory is working, but we have a dog and he IS a hound dog. By this I mean that now that fall has come, this dog can do nothing but hunt. He is trying to be a "people–dog", but his instincts are carrying him off into the woods - he is baying up trees looking for squirrels and chipmunks, anything he can get his paws on to eat! He has been fine all summer long, but as this fall weather comes he has gone crazy. What he was made to be has been exposed! It is all we can do to keep him controlled on a leash.

Why do I tell you this story? It is a picture of me, really, and perhaps you. I am made a certain way and though at times I have obligations (like Chaplain to be a "people-dog"), I find that my true heart - what God has called me to be--is just beneath the surface baying (the "hound dog" term for crying out) to be free. My circumstances hold me in one place, and at one level this is good. But my heart is crying out for something that I am really made for. Let's take a look at some passages that might shed some light on this "what am I really made for" question.

Read Hosea 11:1-4

1. Is this scripture only about God and Israel? Do you think that when God speaks in the Old Testament about His love for His people it is only a love for Israel, or does it extend to us?

When we see and consider the incredible love God had for His people and His call for them to love Him in return, we must remember God is speaking to our hearts and into our lives as well, calling us to be His people, to belong to Him, to love Him and be His beloved children.

There is not an "Old Testament God" and a "New Testament God." There is the God of all creation calling a people to be His own treasured possession. God begins His wooing of us before creation began. Ephesians 1 tells us "God chose us in Him before the creation of the world to be holy and blameless in His sight. In love He predestined us to be adopted as His sons and daughters through Jesus Christ, in accordance with His pleasure and will". Can you let that deep into your heart? Can you let these words replace old words and worn out ideas of people not loving you enough or giving you what you thought you needed? God extends His love to us before we are born and then He waits, like a lover, for us to hear His calling in our lives. These verses in Ephesians have the power to cut every cord of victimization or wounded-ness you are carrying. Allow the God of the Universe to speak these words of love to you: "My child, I've been waiting. I am so pleased you are drawing near to Me. I have seen you and watched your struggles, and I say to you now that I love you and it is My plan and purpose to call you to Myself and to adopt you as My own dear child. Welcome Home."

Read Hosea 10:1; John 15:5; Romans 11:17-24

2. Who does God call "the lush vine"? Who is the Vine in the New Testament?

The Romans passage is very long, (*The Message Translation* is very helpful), but it gives us a clear look at how God views us (as Gentiles, meaning we are not part of the culture or family of Israel) and how we can apply the words of the Old Testament to ourselves. If God loves the Jewish people with an everlasting love, where do we come in? We come in on the side of grace, being called by God. As Romans says, we are grafted into this amazing love of God. We were not part of the "original deal" (the "deal" being the covenant God made with the Israelite people in the Old Testament), so to speak, but Jesus has made a way for us to be one body, even though we are unique individuals in His corporate church.. "In Him there is neither Greek nor Jew, slave nor free, for we are all one in Christ Jesus" (Galatians 3:28). He has become for us the "True Vine," and we are grafted into the family of faith. With this assurance, then, we can look back into the Old Testament and know that the love that God has for the Israelites, He also has for us; the call He has for the Israelites, He now has for us, because we have been "grafted in." Let this knowledge saturate your soul. As Paul reminds us in Ephesians 1, God has called us before the creation of the world to be His very own--His own dear child. As you live your life and go through each day, is this your heart's cry, "I am God's own dear child, and He loves me more than I can ever know?" Does this thought guide you and sustain you, that no matter what happens in your life, you are precious to God and He is wild about you? When our hearts hear this call, day after day, moment after moment, then we are changed…"He loves me, He is wild about me, and He is enthralled by my beauty."

Read Isaiah 62:5 and Zephaniah 3:17

3. If we could truly believe that the God of the universe was "wild about us", what would change for us? What do these scriptures tell you about God's relationship with you?

God has this most precious, tender love for us, and we need to train our ears to hear it, to listen for it, to long for His voice. I believe that is what the Psalmist means when he says, "As the deer pants for the living water so my soul longs after you" (Psalm 42:1). This summer I was traveling to Upstate New York to get the boys from summer camp. It was early, perhaps 6:00 in the morning, and I was following a river through the valley before I headed into the Adirondack Mountains. I turned a bend in the road and there before me was a deer, completely still and having a morning drink in the river. I was so struck by the picture that I kept looking around each bend hoping to see another deer, another reminder of how God wants me to be with Him--seeking Him, receiving Him, resting in Him, quieted by His love. I live so much more like a frightened deer--always with my ears perked up and my tail flying--afraid to be still and quiet. In fact, it is a vivid reminder of the day before my wedding. Kevin, my husband, makes decisions very quickly and getting married was no exception. We met in March and were married in November (our oldest son, Ken, wasn't born until three years later if you were worried!). But I was ready, I knew that God had sent me this man to marry; he loved the Lord and me, so why should I worry? Well, I hadn't forgotten "my people, or my father's house," or my father's words. Since I was a very little girl, I remember my father saying this, "No one will ever love you enough to marry you." The words burned in my heart, seared there by time and repetition. All of Kevin's love and assurance could not match the strong hold these words had on me. So, the day before we were married, I called Kevin and challenged him, "You aren't really going to show up tomorrow?" It was, of course, the cry of a little girl who felt she couldn't be loved, but more than that, it was a test of who I was. I was unlovable, I thought. God sent me a man that, for nineteen years has proved me wrong. But even if he hadn't sent me a husband to meet that deep need, He sent me Himself. Every promise is true; every word of love to me is faithful. My first scripture that I had to know was not John 3:16, it was, "These are the words of the faithful and true" (Revelation 3:14). Before I could believe "Jesus loves me this I know," I *HAD* to know I could trust Him. I had to know He spoke the truth. I had to know He was faithful and to let the truth of God's faithfulness slowly begin to heal the wounds in my soul.

Augustine, who is famous for his <u>Confessions,</u> was an Early Church Father who preached to the church in Northern Africa in the fifth century. He also wrote on interpreting the bible and pastored God's flock for most of his life.

Augustine says this:

> "'And you shall know the truth and the truth shall free you'... Here one may say, 'And what does it profit me to know the truth?' 'And the truth shall free you.' If the truth has no charms for you, let freedom have its charms. In the usage of the Latin tongue, the expression, 'to be free,' is used in two senses; we are used to hearing this word describe one who has escaped danger, or to be rid of some

embarrassment. But the proper use here
of, 'to be free,' is 'to be made free'; just as
'to be saved' is 'to make safe'; 'to be
healed' is 'to be made whole'; so, 'to be
freed' is 'to be made free'." [1]

Augustine's words to me, while complex, offer me
a place to rest. In the truth of God I am literally "made
safe." I am "made free" from my false ideas, from all that
holds me back in wrong thoughts and attitudes. I can find
a resting place here in God's truth because the promise is
that the truth has "made me free". I am free then, to love
God passionately for I no longer am bound by my sin, my
hurt, other's sin, and others' sins against me. I can take all
these to Christ and know, once and for all, that these are
washed away. I am cleansed from all unrighteousness--
not some, not a little. Every unrighteous act of mine or
those done against me is cleansed by Christ's blood.
When I look at my own heart and the wounds that hold
me, they all find a place of healing in the One who has
come to save and free me. I am again the captive in
Deuteronomy who needs to be taken out of captivity and
made into a bride. The truth that I am loved is the key to
my freedom. Just as grief was the key to receiving the
comfort of God, now truth is the key to receiving the love
of God, because God is love and now to receive His love,
I have only to believe. The key is to tell myself the truth.
For the longest time I really refused to "be" a child of
God. I know this seems ridiculous, but my logic went
something like this: "Being a child isn't a safe thing given
my past, so I won't be God's child, I'll be His slave, His
servant or anything else, but God, PLEASE, don't ask me
to be Your *child*." If you have read 1 John you know Paul
refers to us as, "dear children," or "my dear children," or
even, "you, dear children, are from God" (1 John 4:4).
This was truth, but my wounded heart could not embrace

it. Once I accepted the Lord's Words over my own wounds, healing began. I could say, "Yes, I am a child of God." "Yes, God loves me." I didn't have to continue on with my tortured way of thinking, I had to be freed from the past and sin and made safe by salvation. God in His grace has taken care of the rest. His truth is the key to my love for Him. Once I accepted His word as truth, then I could begin to realign my faulty, harmful thinking. It hasn't been easy, but the wounds I received as a child slowly have faded in the light of His truth. As Augustine says, I am "made safe" and "made free"--God's work of love done on our behalf.

Read Deuteronomy 7:8, 9

4. What holds you? What wounds or hurts keep you from trusting God's heart of love toward you?

What does scripture say about God's love and faithfulness? Which holds greater weight in your heart, God's love and faithfulness or the depth of your wounds? Do the wounds and hurts in your life minimize God's love and faithfulness? How? You can skip over these questions or you can begin to allow God to deal with some of your hurts by acknowledging them to Him. He already knows what wounds you, but by saying the words out loud, speaking them in prayer their power is diminished. Once I say, "God, what that friend said really hurt", I have already gained perspective: "Oh, it's just someone's words-- it does not necessarily reflect the truth". When I leave words and wounds in my head and heart, they gain a strong hold on me because I do not always test their truthfulness. I might brood over them, turn them around, over and over again, but I might never ask myself, "Is this true?" When I pray, when I tell God of the hurts, frustrations and anger I feel, He sheds His light and truth on them and I do not sit in the darkness of my thoughts or feelings as long. My thoughts and perceptions are often the things that keep me from trusting God's heart of love toward me.

Read Deuteronomy 6:20-23

5. If Egypt in the Old Testament is a picture of "where we have come from" in terms of our life in the world, has God "delivered you from Egypt" or redeemed you from the house of bondage? Can you honestly say that there is nothing that is hindering you from receiving God's love and His call on your life?

Remember our dog Chaplain? He was made to be a hunter. Every morning now he wakes with his nose in the air and a little bit of wag in his tail. He runs from door to door and bays to be let out, to taste the freedom of the hunt and the smell of the woods (have you ever heard a hound dog baying?…it is a pitiful sound!). He longs to be chasing something! But every morning I hinder him. I put him on a leash and torture him with a brisk walk around the pond. He wants to run free, but I have him bound. He wants to give chase, but I want him by my side. His greater, grander purpose is to chase and hunt. All I have for him is a leash!

We are made for a greater purpose than "getting through the day." We are even made for a grander purpose than finding God's will and doing it. I say that with fear and trepidation, but our grandest purpose, I believe, is to be loved by God-- to be wooed and courted and pursued by a passionate God that refuses to settle for our luke-warm religion. He wants us to wake longing for Him. He longs for us and has given us a Book full of love stories to prove it. Like the examples in the Old Testament, He is our "Hosea", and we are "Gomer", the ever adulterous wife. We are the Shulamite bride, and He is the King pursuing us. Over and over in the New Testament Paul tells us that we are the "Bride of Heaven." We are Christ's bride and the Old Testament gives us the rare picture of us being courted by God. We need to understand God passionately loves us, and no matter what we have or have not been through, there is Someone who desires us. God loves us and cares for us. In Isaiah 54:5 He actually calls Himself "our Husband." The call on our lives is to be united with our Maker. God actually says this.

Read Isaiah 54:1-8

6. What part of this scripture, if any, most reflects your life right now?

Do you relate to any of the feelings Isaiah is expressing: fear, humiliation, shame, reproach, one forsaken, and one grieving? God's great compassion and mercies are new every morning, but there is something very interesting about them--they need to be experienced. Just like the deer that chooses stillness in the cool of the morning, we need to choose to sit at God's feet, to soak in His word, to bask in His love. The Psalmists are so adept at this. They go through valleys and mountain top experiences, but their bedrock faith is in God's goodness and His love. I wonder if my mode of operating is based solely on God's goodness and love to me. God calls Himself our Maker and our Husband; this is not a "God far-off." This is a God who is passionate about us and longs to know us in the most intimate ways. He longs to know you and love you as only your Maker can. Isn't it fascinating that God calls Himself our Maker first… sometimes we feel that nagging, "if people only knew me as I really am, they wouldn't love me." But here is God, our Maker, saying "I know you and I made you; I love you and long to have you love and trust Me."

Read Psalm 145:13-18

7. Do I believe I was made to be loved?

Here is the heart of the matter. Just as our hound dog is "made" to hunt, so I am "made" to be loved. No matter what has or hasn't happened in my life, do I believe with all my heart that I was made by God to be loved by Him? Just as we put Chaplain on a leash and hinder him from being what he was born to be, sometimes our life experiences or our disappointments with God or others have led us to believe that we are not worthy or able or entitled to be loved. But God's word tells us He is "loving towards all He has made" (verse 13). Are there things in your life that hinder you from knowing that God loves you? What experiences or beliefs about yourself or others do you hold that cause you to think, "I'm not worthy of love or I don't deserve love?" Is there anything holding you back from being whom God made you to be--His precious bride, His beloved child? Can you really accept in your heart the unconditional love of God? God loves us. It is as simple as this. He calls us and woos us and wants to be close to us. We can "do" all the right things religiously (go to church, attend or lead Bible studies), but God asks us to *be,* be loved, to be "beloved."

"Be here--the King is wild for you" (Psalm 45:11).

How are you living your life? Are you "here"? Are you able to hear the Lord's gentle Voice of Love? Are you able to recognize how much He desires you? Do you remember when you first fell in love? You couldn't wait to "be" with the other person. Their very presence was all you needed to feel complete, to feel joy, to feel fulfilled. Really, when the Psalmist asks us to "be here", what he is really saying is, "Don't you want to be with Him? Wouldn't you rather be here with God than anywhere else? Don't let anything hinder you from "being" with God--being available to be loved by Him, still enough to catch the whisper of His tender voice of love and mercy. Clear your thoughts, your calendar and your heart of all other longings, and let the God of the

Universe love you and hold you. This is what He wants.

"Lord, you know our hearts; you know where we are hurting and what holds us back from being close to You. Could you please hold us, Lord? Calm our fears, melt our sadness, wrap us in your love and give us the assurance of Your tender mercy."

Chapter 3

Called to Honor Him

"Listen, O Daughter, consider and give ear; forget your people and your father's house. The King is enthralled by your beauty; honor Him, for He is your Lord" (Psalm 45:10, 11).

Once we have established in our hearts that the King is enthralled by our beauty we have a few decisions to make. If we imagine ourselves to be the captive who has mourned in the King's house and now we come to understand that we are captivating, how do we respond? In the Old Testament book of Esther we have a story of a captive girl made queen.

Read Esther 2:5-18

1. Do we honor God with our presence as Esther honored the king of Persia?

Imagine yourself, for a moment, as Esther. You are a gorgeous girl who has caught the attention of those looking for a new queen. You suspected you were beautiful and now it has been confirmed, because you are gathered up with all the other beautiful girls and taken to

the king's palace. You know you are a foreigner in this
land of Persia, but you really didn't have time to tell those
who were gathering the virgins. You might have
protested, but you might also have been inwardly thrilled
to be chosen as one of the beautiful in the land. You are
here now, being prepared in the king's palace with beauty
treatments (think spas!) It is your turn to go to the king;
you have been summoned. Everyone has heard the story
of the previous Queen, Vashti, and how she refused to go
to the king when she was called, how she didn't honor the
king with her presence. You are a little afraid, yet you go
with nothing to offer but yourself. You are only a captive
in a foreign king's land, but you will be obedient, you will
honor this king because you know your God has never
failed you in all these years of living in this foreign land.
Your beauty is captivating and surely, the king will be
enthralled by your beauty. You become the king's
favorite and find that God Himself, the God of your
people, has blessed you and uses you in amazing ways to
save your own people. (Read the rest of Esther if you
want to know all the details!)

Esther honored a foreign king and God used her
mightily. Think of the story of Esther and imagine a
willful, stubborn girl who refuses to go to the king. What
will happen to her? Surely she will not win the king's
favor, she will not bring him honor. Can we look at our
own spiritual journey with God and recognize that He is
our King and we are to honor Him, to choose to hear His
call of, "forget your people and your father's house, I'm
wild about you!" (Psalm 45:11; *The Message Translation*)
When God calls to us "be here!" it is to be with Him.
Psalm 84:10 says, "Better is one day in your courts than
thousands elsewhere." The Psalmist loves to be in God's
presence. Do we? We honor Him by spending time with

Him. Do we honor God with our time and with the way in which we respond to His call to "be here"?

Read Psalm 100: 1-5

2. Do we believe the Psalmist's words that the Lord's love endures forever? Has the belief in God's love reached our hearts?

Let's say we have been an "Esther." We have come into the King's house a captive and now we are His bride. We have acknowledged the King's goodness and the King's love, and now what? Do we spend time loving God and being loved by Him or do we just read about His love and not truly let it touch the places in our hearts that need His love? God's word is shockingly clear when He says He is wild about us. His love is spilled all over the pages of the Bible, spilled on Calvary, spilled throughout all of history as God continues to woo and to call us to Himself.

I have a dear friend whom I haven't seen in over a year and the family came to visit. They got out of their car after a long journey and this friend ran right into my arms! I was so overwhelmed by her display of affection! How much more so will I be overwhelmed by My Father's love? He loves me with an unconditional and steadfast love, and He calls me as His bride. Can I even fathom the love He has for me, how wide and high and deep? Often, though, I am unaffected by this deep love; I don't let God's deep, abiding and faithful love for me fill me with joy, honor and love for him. I try my best to "do" the things God asks me to do, but I don't really let

Him near my heart. I keep a little list of things I must do for God, but I fail to see He is after me! He wants my heart; I try to give Him a set little quiet time. He wants my will; I give Him my money. He wants my soul and mind; I give Him my "to do" list, all neatly checked off for Him. God is so faithful to me, but He longs to have me close enough to hear His voice.

Read Matthew 15:7-9

3. What can it mean for us to honor God?

Jesus is quoting the Old Testament prophet Isaiah, and he makes it very clear that our hearts have to be involved if we are to truly honor God. There is more to honoring God than saying we honor Him. We can "say" just about anything, but the question is really more about our hearts than our words, more about our intentions than our actions. Jesus wants our hearts involved when we are honoring Him. Is your heart free to be involved in worshipping the Lord? Where is your heart, where is my heart? If I have mourned in my Father's house I am a little freer to love my Lord and King. If I have been at His feet and shared with Him, then my heart is close to Him. This is what God wants: a people to love, a people that "love Him with all their hearts and souls and minds and strength" (Matthew 22:37). I remember once telling God in prayer," God, I can't love you with my whole heart, it is wounded; I can't love you with my mind, it is cluttered; I can't love you with my whole soul, it is shattered; and I can't love you with all my strength because I am so weary." Now, so much of that is not right thinking, but there are grains of truth. What I needed to know is that

Jesus would bind up my broken heart, free my mind, rescue my soul and would give me the strength I needed; but first, I had to come to Him. Sometimes, our view of who we are keeps us from God. That was the case with me: "God, I'm not worthy to be in Your presence. I can't even share with You all that I am because I am so awful." My heart was crushed with sorrow and sadness; yours may not be; your heart may just be busy and distracted, only you can know. The good news is God knows our hearts and our frailties and He so lovingly corrects us. Other times it is our view of God that hinders us from coming to Him. We need a correct view of God as we approach Him. He is our Lord, yet He is our Maker and our Sustainer. He is the One who calls us out of darkness and into His marvelous light. He calls us into a relationship of love. The move from darkness to light needs to be complete. Any shadows we have left in our soul from pain or loss need to come into His marvelous light. All of our thinking about God and living in relationship to Him and others needs to be light and love and freedom. Our hearts need to be free and flooded with His glorious light- even though we might have suffered along the way or still suffer today. Find your heart- it may be "wounded," it may be frozen in rage, it may just be distracted. You are the only one who can recover your heart. Find a place where you can be quiet and ask the Lord this question:

"God, where is my heart? Is it open and free to love You and others? Is it filled with pain and crushed by adversity? Is it numb and unavailable to You?" We can say anything about loving God, but loving involves our hearts. Allow God access to your heart: wounded, whole, crushed, weighed down, wherever your heart is; there is One who has come to mend your broken heart and free you to be loved and to love.

John Chrysostom writes,

> "For this house (The Church) is a spiritual
> surgery, that whatever wounds we may
> have received outside, here we may heal,
> not gather fresh ones to take with us. Yet
> if we do not give heed to the Spirit
> speaking to us, we shall not only fail to
> clear ourselves of our former hurts, but
> shall get others in addition." [1]

Read Psalm 95:1-7

**4. What does the psalmist say the Lord is? What are
we asked to do in verse six?**

When we "bow down" to someone we are paying
them respect and honor. We are acknowledging their
worthiness and their authority or right to be given honor.
Webster's Dictionary defines "to bow" as to: "to bend the
head or knee in reverence, respect, submission or
salutation." We do not honor God with words only, we
honor Him with the way we carry ourselves in His
presence. We can say, as the Israelites of old, that we love
God and worship Him, but if we have not "bended the
knee in reverence and submission," then it does not matter
what we say. Honor is a bended knee and surrendered
heart. Our hearts determine whether or not we are
honoring God, not our words. When our hearts are open
to God, when pain has been mourned and we have enough
room for God to meet us there, we find He is a most
enjoyable guest. If our hearts are filled with daily worries

and distractions, if our minds are racing with our own agenda, whether it godly is or not, we will find there is very little space there for God to dwell. It is a little like the garden I made last year. I filled the back yard with beautiful flowerbeds and berry patches. There were all kinds of gatherings of flowers and bushes that bloomed with an incredible fragrance, but no where was there a seat. I had not one bench or seat or "nook" in which to enjoy the gorgeous hibiscus and sedum, strawberries and raspberries. A friend pointed it out to me, "Diane, where do you sit down to enjoy the garden?" Oh, enjoy the garden? I'd never thought of that. I'd been so busy planting and weeding, pruning and cultivating. I never considered resting here. In a way, that is very much like our relationship with God at times. I will do almost anything for Him, but to rest and sit in His presence is a whole different ballgame. I don't know these rules, I don't know how to play, all I know is how to "do things for God," rather than sitting with Him and enjoying Him. Now I have a bench in my garden and a place on a stone step where I can soak in the sunshine each morning. I can rest there, reflect, dream, scheme, I can just "be." God longs to be with us in this way, for us to honor Him with our presence, to be an "Esther" who chooses to obey the King's summons.

Read Hebrews 10:22-25

5. Have there been times in your life you have felt the Lord calling you to be near to Him, but you have not drawn near? What distractions or wounds prevent you from drawing near to God?

When we can be "real" with God and have confidence in Him, we will find bold entrance into His chambers. We have a bride getting ready, remember. There is also the bridegroom, waiting; ready for a relationship and intimacy. We honor God when we come to Him in authenticity and with confidence in Who He is and what He is able to do in and for us. God is calling us to honor Him with our presence. True intimacy requires bringing my real self to the relationship and confidence in the other to receive me. Do I do this with God, or do I show up with a list of requests for myself, my family or my friends? God longs to have me honor Him and I am most busy talking at Him. The issue here is truly, do we know ourselves? Are we aware of all that simmers below the polite interactions with God and others? "God is greater than our hearts and He knows everything" (1 John 3:20). So it is by faith we enter this most Holy place of communion with God. We come and listen. We come and allow the infinite love of God to shape us and heal us. We draw near to God by simply walking into His presence with great joy and confidence because of Christ's work on the cross, but we also might draw near broken and wounded. And still, the God of all creation waits for us, arms open wide asking only that we come. Come with a sincere heart; the God of heaven cannot be played false. Come with full assurance of faith: faith in Who God is and faith in what He can do in and through us. You see, God longs to work in us in a way that brings others to Him. "Let us consider how we can spur one another on to love and good deeds" (verse 24). God's work in us heals us and draws others in as well. When God "sprinkles our hearts clean" we find they are open, refreshed, and perhaps even ready for relationship with others! Hearts made whole in God's presence have a refreshing affect on the world! Allow your heart to reach out to others in consideration and encouragement. When our hearts are sprinkled and our bodies washed there is a sense of refreshment and wholeness. Refresh others as well!

Read 1 John 1:9

6. Is wholeness and cleansing a daily experience for you with God? If not, why not? Can one approach a holy God without first being cleansed by Christ?

John Chrysostom writes this:

> "Hearken, O Daughter. She was first a daughter of demons, a daughter of the earth, unworthy of the earth and now she has become the daughter of the King. And this He wished who loved her. For He saw one who was uncomely and He makes her young, not having spot or wrinkle. Oh what a bridegroom adorning with grace the ungracefulness of His bride. Since the dowry depends on hearing (hearken) what is hearing but faith (faith comes by hearing and hearing by the word of God.) What did He give the bride in her dowry? He gave her forgiveness of sins, remission of punishment, righteousness, sanctification, redemption." [2]

All of these qualities are the same ones spoken of in Hebrews where the scripture refers to our hearts needing to be sincere (true faith), sprinkled clean from a guilty conscience and our bodies washed with pure water. Chrysostom reminds us of the power of the love of God. God wishes to call us into His presence because He loves us and He pours His grace upon us and this gives us a gracefulness we could not have on our own. God asks us to receive the dowry of love and forgiveness and righteousness. He gives us gifts of being made holy (sanctification) and redemption (being bought or freed from whatever distresses.) These are not gifts to scoff at or overlook. These are the gifts from the King of Kings that have the power to change us and change our world. These are "identity" gifts. We are being given a whole new identity. Like the "Daughter" Chrysostom portrays: "First she was a daughter of demons... now she is a daughter of the King." Fill in your name, or the names you have been called, or the names you have called yourself: First I was... now I am... God longs to have you identify yourself as His child. Do not miss the powerful, life-changing identity that He has for you. Accept the dowry, listen for His love and then respond in faith.

We are to come before God, honor Him, and bend our knee before our Maker because that is who we are. We are His children. He is a worthy King who has attributed to us the honors and privileges of life in the court. We are required to enter certain places wearing certain garments. Rags will not suffice here. So, if you are wearing rags in your heart because you still somehow see yourself as a beggar, be done with it. This King accepts no lowly servants; He promptly makes them His children as long as they have ears to hear His call on their lives. It is almost as if the "common people" are at the King's gate and He says to them, if you will be my own dear child, and then please, step over here, my Son has a garment for you fitting for the palace. Take the garment of righteousness, child, and become Mine and honor Me, for I am your King!

When we were in Scotland, we saw the Edinburgh Castle. Interestingly enough, the castle is also a fortress. This is true of God as well, for He is our fortress and a very strong tower. He calls us to be the bride of the King and the way we honor God in this world is first to have a sincere heart that desires to be close to Him. But then, we must fight with all our might to live a life that is worthy of the King. We are called to the battle lines to defend our faith, we are called to feed the hungry, clothe the naked, shelter the weary, and we are also called to live our lives in a manner worthy of our calling. We have a King to represent, a battle for our souls in which we must be diligent and aware, finding ourselves good comrades and loyal companions and clinging to our King through it all. To live a godly life is to bring honor to the King. He is our Lord and we must follow not only His call, but His example. "Follow my example as I follow the example of Christ," says Paul in 1 Corinthians 11:1.

Read Psalm 90:1; Psalm 91:1, 2

7. Where are you residing right now?

It is a curious question, but we can be living in a certain place, yet not dwelling where we belong. The best illustration I have is of a palace in Germany called Benrath Palace. I visited there and found the most amazing "house for pleasurable pursuits", a summer home for a wealthy family. The interesting fact is that the family's main residence was in Manheim, Germany and the owner of the palace visited there for five hours one day while it was under construction. Do not miss the spiritual parallel for us; we have been given and promised a place to dwell: in the shadow of the Almighty, in the Lord's presence, but we do not visit often. We are under construction, just like the summer home built for pleasure, and God calls us to come and dwell with Him, but we are often busy, often preoccupied with our worldly obligations and responsibilities. God is offering a place to rest; what will we choose? There will always be a world full of pressure and circumstances that are beyond our strength, but will we choose to dwell with God; will we come under the shelter of the Almighty? We have a dwelling place, will we stop the pace and race of our lives long enough to rest? Will we choose rest and pleasure in God's presence, or will we choose the pull of the world? I can appear to be living close to God, but my heart and life must match up. I need to ask myself if I am really living close to God, resting in Him, refreshed by Him, having an inner quiet that fills and frees me from this hectic life. There is a place, a palace perhaps, waiting for you and a Lord, most willing to refresh you.

"God, you know our hearts and how we long to be with You, yet we are often times pressed and perhaps wounded by the pressures and experiences of this life. Would You woo us, call us into Your presence and refresh us there? Give us hearts that know You and honor You. Keep us, Lord in Your love that we might know our true identity in You. Be our safe shelter. Amen."

Chapter 4

Called to be Glorious

"Listen, O daughter, consider and give ear: Forget your people and your father's house. The King is enthralled by your beauty; honor Him, for He is your Lord. The Daughter of Tyre will come with a gift; men of wealth will seek your favor. All glorious is the princess within her chamber" (Psalm 45:10-13).

This is clearly a bride getting ready. This is a woman who knows she is loved and cherished and who is already receiving all the pre-wedding gifts. Can you see her, in her room, preparing? All the outward show of celebration is there, but internally and within her own chamber the bride readies herself. I want to consider this question in our study: Are we glorious? Do we see ourselves as glorious? How does God view us? At times we are unaware that how we view ourselves has a direct affect on how we relate to God. Our image of who we are needs to come from truth and we can find that truth in God's word.

Read Psalm 8:3-9; Psalm 4:6

1. Where in the scheme of God's created order is man found? What does he then say about us? What are we crowned with?

We are created and formed with a stamp of God's glory. It is there because we are all created in the image of God. When you look across the table when you are at lunch with a friend or having dinner with your spouse, you are seeing a reflection of the glory of the Lord. No matter how different or downcast or wounded a person may be, they have a flicker of glory living in them just by the virtue of the one Who made them. We were created *by* glory *for* glory. Every part of our lives is a place to shine.

I have an old ring of my mother's. It came in to my possession quite miraculously after my mother died. All her personal belongings had long been discarded, but after her husband died I was encouraged to come and look through his home to see if there was anything of my mom's left there. Sure enough, in an old wooden box I found a ring with no stone in it. It was bent and dented a little, but it was all I found of my Mother's jewelry. I took the ring, my husband saying, "Are you sure you want that old thing?" I did. I took it to a jeweler and much to my surprise, I found that the ring was solid gold and all I needed to do was choose a stone. I wanted something that would honor my mom, something to remind me of how precious she was. I chose an amethyst. It was a beautiful purple stone which reminded me that my Mom was made by the King of Kings. She was beautiful to Him because she was created by Him. I didn't see much glory in her life, but I think there was One who knew her far better than I, who treasured her beyond belief. I'm not sure she even knew about His love, but His love was real for her none the less. I want to spend my life knowing I am precious to God, knowing He is wild about me, knowing that I am glorious in His eyes. I want to need no other person's approval because I am so convinced of my Savior's love for me. I have that amethyst ring still and it reminds me that not only am I my mother's daughter (the outside of the ring was hers) but I am also a daughter of the King (a royal stone fills the heart of that ring.) I am always God's child. He looks at us and sees the glory He has given us in creation, and also the glory He longs to bring to us through life in His Son. There is no other identity that trumps this. We are His. I can let my life be identified however I choose, but the reality is that I am God's creation, crowned with glory and honor. I am not a lowly servant; I am not a child begging to belong. We are all God's beloved, who He has called out and conferred with honor. If we could settle our status with God, our relationship with Him, with ourselves and others would be vastly improved! God wants to fit us for His glory.

Read Mark 5:25-34

2. How did Jesus' presence and this woman's pursuit of Him bring her glory?"

This is a desperate woman who needs her life changed, fixed, something done! As it is, she is an outcast in her society because of her "issue of blood." She has a physical issue that has kept her from intimacy and relationships. God's glory is no where to be seen in her as she hangs her head in shame and her body is drained of its strength. Her condition is outward. *She* does not reflect God's glory- do we? Do we live our lives as though we have been made by the creator of the Universe, as though He has chosen us for His own purposes or plans, or do we live with issues, afraid to be all God has called us to be? Are we afraid that others have ruined us, ruined our chances to be what God wants? Are we certain that our lives can never be the same because something happened, someone did something, God didn't do something, give something? Can we live pursuing God even though we are disappointed, desperate, disillusioned? Sometimes we are in such pain that we isolate ourselves. We are overwhelmed and cannot fathom pursuing anyone or anything. This is our point of desperation. This is when we need to reach out our hand and just touch the hem of His garment. God is waiting for us to reach out. He longs to touch us with His presence and His power; He longs to bestow glory on us.

Listen to John Chrysostom's words:

> "For though she was bound by her affliction, yet her faith had given her wings. And mark how He comforts her, saying, 'Your faith has saved you.' Now surely had He drawn her forward for display...He did this with the intention of glorifying her and to amend others, and not to show Himself glorious...For this cause He brought her forward, and proclaimed her praise, and cast out her fear (for 'she came,' it is said, 'trembling.') and He caused her to be of good courage, and together with health of body, He gave her also other provision for her journey, in that

He said, 'Go in peace'."[1]

Let us ask God to give us a faith that propels us to Him, that He might touch us with His presence and give our hearts courage and peace. When God is at work in our desperate circumstances we find that we are changed and those around us have their faith changed as well, because God "amends" them, amends their wrong ideas and misconceptions of who He is and who they are. It is like the man born blind. When the Pharisees ask, in John Chapter 9: "Who sinned, this man or his parents?" Jesus touches the man and heals him, but He also corrects their wrong thinking. "No one sinned; it was so that the glory of God could be revealed in him." These are strong words. We want to (and should) give God glory, but God also asks us to live lives that are glorious by our very connection with Him. When we live in a way that others know we have been in God's presence, then He receives glory. If we carry courage and peace on our journey, we bring God glory and we may help another whose faith is not so strong. Dare we do this, living from a strong connection with God and allowing Him to give us courage and healing?

Read 2 Corinthians 3:6-18

3. What is the condition of reflecting God's glory? What does it mean to you to have your face unveiled?

In this passage of scripture we are shown a picture of what it was like for the Israelite people when Moses came down from the mountain with the Ten Commandments. Remember Moses had spent forty days and forty nights on a mountain top with God. He had received God's laws for God's people and he was unaware that his face shone with an intense brightness which was God's glory. We have now received a ministry of the Holy Spirit, which is Christ reconciling to Himself all who will call on His Name, and not only reconciling, but making righteous and giving His Spirit as well. This is the glory that is talked about in these verses. In verse sixteen it says, "But whenever anyone turns to the Lord, the veil is taken away. Now the Lord is the Spirit and where the Spirit of the Lord is, there is freedom. And we, who with unveiled faces all reflect the Lord' glory, are being transformed into His likeness with an ever-increasing glory, which comes from the Lord, who is the Spirit."

I think of this process of "unveiling our faces" like a spa treatment. Have you ever had a facial? You are completely pampered and wrapped in this feeling of being cared for and nurtured and then the treatment begins, the layers are stripped away. We are made to see that there are contaminants and environmental pollutants that have dulled our skin and caused damage to the cells. Old layers of dead cells are stripped away as a new layer of skin is exposed and found to be radiant. Environmental exposure has tainted our skin, but we are shown a way to be cleansed from these toxins and made to look and feel and reflect beauty. This is so true for our hearts and souls as well. We are living in a fallen, tainted, contaminated world. Our lives, our families, friends and spouses all contribute to a feeling of covering up at times. We are made to feel we need to "just keep going" when in fact what we need is to have a good long cry or to soak in God's presence so that we might free our hearts from its hurts and wounds and disappointments. Instead of "unveiling" our faces, we cover up our deep hurts and pain with a mask. It is time to go into our chambers for a beauty treatment. Ask the Lord of your heart, who is the Spirit, to teach you all things- if your face isn't radiant with the Lord's glory, perhaps there are things in your heart or life that are "covering up" the Lord's glory or presence? Is there something that is holding you back from knowing and sensing His presence and the warmth of His countenance shining down upon you? We live in a state of grace. Nothing we do or do not do can remove the Lord's love from us, nothing that happens to us can separate us from God's love (see Romans 8:35-39).

Read 1 Corinthians 10:31; 2 Corinthians 3:16-18

4. Is my life reflecting God's glory?

What we hold onto in this earthly life may act like a veil that covers our faces and our hearts; what we cling to with clenched fists may be the very thing that keeps us from experiencing the glory of God in our lives. How can we know if this is true for us? There is a simple guide in this passage in 2 Corinthians: "Where the Spirit of the Lord is, there is freedom." God's Spirit brings us truth and teaches us about God. He reminds us of all that God and His Word tell us, yet it requires attentiveness to listen to God's Spirit and walk in that freedom. We have freedom with God when we are able to share our hearts with Him, spend time with Him and experience His love

for us. We have freedom with others when we can be
ourselves, share our gifts and reflect the Lord's love to
them. If we are caught in the trap of needing approval or
value or worth from someone other than God, then we
might want to consider what "veils" we are wearing. A
"veil" is simply something that separates us from the
Lord, ourselves and others. It can be an action (sin will
do that every time) it may be an attitude, and again sinful
ones like pride or bitterness or resentment, or it may be a
belief that we hold that isn't true. Mine are most often
beliefs, things like, "God can't love me because: (fill in
the blank for the day) I lost my temper, I'm worthless,
I'm hopeless, and I'm useless. Or, "If God loved me He
would (fill in your own blank) "change my husband,
change my kids, change me, change my situation, and
give me purpose…." The problem with these kinds of
feelings on a day-to-day basis is that my thinking doesn't
reflect what God says is true about me. I have trouble
walking in the freedom of God's Spirit because, "Where
the Spirit of the Lord is, there is freedom." Jesus calls the
Spirit the "Spirit of truth." This truth is the key to our
understanding of reflecting God's glory and living in
freedom because when Jesus comes to bring us the truth,
He says it will set us free. Sometimes, our job is to look
at what we believe or think and ask ourselves hard
questions, like: "Is what I am thinking reflecting God's
truth about me, about God, about God's love for me, and
about others and their influence upon me?" When I can
begin to engage myself in a conversation about truth- not
how I feel or what I think - then the transforming power
of Jesus' words will be evident in my life: "You shall
know the truth and the truth will set you free" (John 8:32).
God offers us an unconditional love and we do not always
accept that. We place conditions on ourselves and on
God that blur the truth of what He declares in His word.
"God, I know you love me when my life looks a certain

way. God, I'll be able to accept Your love when You explain to me why things happened in my life. God, You couldn't love me because..." (fill in your own blank). These are all lies we tell ourselves and we keep ourselves from the truth of God's love and the freedom He offers us.

Can you say that you accept or are beginning to accept God's unconditional love for you? Do you know in your heart of hearts that God's love for you is real, that it fills you and that you are His precious child, a child of the King? Again, we will find that these truths would change our lives if we would let them. Our sense of worth and esteem would flow from the knowledge that we are glorious in God's eyes. Paul says of the Thessalonians in 1 Thessalonians 2:20, "You are our glory and our joy". This is said of believers who have accepted God's Word and grow in it. We need to be reminded that our Father loves us and desires for us to live from that truth. It is our foundation. Think back to the spa treatment for a moment and say that all the impurities from living in this world have been washed away (the Christian's "bar of soap," 1 John 1:9) We have been cleansed from all unrighteousness, so now, what is next? We are to put on a foundation and that foundation is the love that God has for you. We are to soak in the truth of God's love for us and let it sink into our very hearts and souls so that we might reflect the Lord's glory.

Read Colossians 1:19-27

5. What has been reconciled to Christ? Who has been reconciled to Christ? How do we appear in Christ's

sight? What is our hope of glory?

Christ has come to reconcile us to Himself and remove every blemish, spot and accusation. We are no longer living under the weight of worldly contamination, but we are made holy in His sight. Is this how we live? Do we live in a way that reflects our holiness? These are hard questions, but as the verses continue on you see that Paul reminds us to "continue in the faith." We must have the assurance, stand before the mirror in our inner chamber, and know that Christ lives in us. There is no other way to reflect His glory and to live a holy life; if I do not know for certain that Christ lives in me, perhaps I need to return to the basics of my faith. When we have been assured of our standing before God, knowing that we have been called, reconciled, loved, cherished, then we find we cannot contain it! We cling to the hope that is held out in the gospel. We have a hope that we can share and we find ourselves engaged in the process of reconciling others. We desire to see others share in the truths of our faith and the freedom and love God calls us to. What a calling, knowing that we have the privilege of sharing with others Christ's reconciliation!

Read 2 Corinthians 4:7-11

6. What is the treasure we hold? What kind of vessel holds this treasure? What is to be revealed in our bodies?

The life of Christ needs to be seen in and through us. When we feel crushed, perplexed, weighed down, or abandoned, this is the time to remember who lives in us. We do not carry around in us some ineffective, uncaring, or unseeing God; we carry around in us The Christ, The Holy One from God. The all-surpassing power that we need in our lives is available to us because Christ lives in us; this is our hope. The all-surpassing power of God dwells within us: do we believe this? When all about us we find ourselves completely overwhelmed, we can know that the life of Jesus can still be revealed in us whatever the circumstances. If I could choose to live from the place of power and position that God has given me, I would find I view my circumstances as just that: circumstances. God is giving me an opportunity to let His power and His life work in and through me. The more difficult the circumstance, the more I cling. I can ask God to take me as His vessel and fill me with Himself. This would be life changing if in the moment of my crushing trials I would look up to God and say, "Could *You* do this? I'm not able, but I know You are able and You are living in me, so, could *You* take over now?" I can be so self-reliant, so sure that I need to be strong and take care of things and yet God is waiting for me to say, "Help!"

When our children were very small I had run out of dishwasher soap; it was late in the day and I didn't want to run to the store to get any, so I put dish soap in the dishwasher. I know, it wasn't the best move I have ever made, but I thought a little bit might be alright. For a few minutes things were fine, but then huge bubbles started flowing from the dishwasher. Soon, the whole kitchen floor was covered in bubbles. I had three small boys watching me, waiting for my reaction, and I just remember saying, "Lord, help!" This is still what I need to do: cry, "Lord, help!" I try to live life my own way, on my own strength, with my own ideas and God is waiting for me to say, "Help." Will I call to Him or will I keep filling my life and heart and mind with my own solutions? His power is made perfect in my weakness: can I admit I am weak and need help?

Read Ephesians 3:14-21

7. In what am I to be rooted and established? With what am I to be filled?

Consider your "inner being" your inner chamber. "All glorious is the princess in her chamber." (Psalm 45) If we can get that straight, that first and foremost we must know in our inner being, in our inner chamber, that we are the "bride of heaven" that we are the "apple of God's eye," then we can go forth with confidence and assurance that we are glorious and bring God glory in this world. Are you rooted and established in God's love, or are there weeds of concern and anxiety that are choking the love of God out of the garden of your heart? Is there room in your heart for Christ to dwell, or are there some "veils" that need to be removed? Are you filled to the measure of all the fullness of God, or are other worries filling your heart? Here is the real truth to grasp…"God is able to do immeasurably more than all you can ask or imagine, according to His power that is at work within us- to Him be glory in the church and in Christ Jesus" (Ephesians 3:20, 21).

      What happens in my inner chamber matters. All my hurts and wounds and doubts and despair are an opportunity to reflect glory, because I cannot depend on my own strength to "get by" or "get through it" or "make it." I have to rely on God. I have to trust His magnificent love for me. I must open my hands to accept gifts from afar- gifts of grace and mercy, comfort and hope. All these come to me as a bride of the King. And finally, as I prepare myself in my chamber, God has to be enough for me. I need to be able to let go of all the other loves in my life and let God be the one who meets my deepest longings for love. Perhaps He will restore those things we feel the locust has eaten (Joel 2:25) and perhaps He won't, but we can choose to say with Job, "Though He slay me, yet will I hope in Him" (Job 13:15). I must remember that it is, "Christ in me, the hope of glory," that is my call. I am not my own, I am God's. Once I chose to follow Him it was as if a veil was lifted as 2 Corinthians says, and now it is my privilege to keep the veil from my face, to live in a way that I can reflect God's glory. It is almost like choosing to put a precious stone into a gold ring. I could have left the ring at my step-father's house; I could have been left in sin. My love for my mother drew me to "rescue" that ring; God's love for me drew Him to rescue me. Then, I could have left the ring in its broken state; I could have been left without hope and a future. I might have chosen to have the ring cleaned up, but not have the precious stone replaced; I could have been taken from sin and given a future, but not fully comprehended my identity in Christ and that it is: "Christ in me, the hope of glory" (Colossians 1:27). That knowledge fills my days and my life with purpose and meaning. We let so many things in our lives identify us; what would happen if we let our identity come from the truth that God loves us and longs to dwell in us and have His glory shine through us? What glory could be revealed in my life and in the church if I would continue to strive to be "all glorious, a princess within my chamber?"

"Lord, you know our hearts. If there are things in our hearts and lives right now that are keeping us from reflecting your glory, please Lord, send your Spirit and teach us. Show us what needs to be removed from our heart and our life so that we might walk with you and spend time with you, being in your presence and knowing your love. May we be open to your Spirit, as you long to live in us and be revealed in us."

Chapter 5

Called to Be Dressed

"Listen, O daughter, consider and give ear; forget your people and your father's house. The King is enthralled by your beauty; honor Him, for He is your Lord. The Daughter of Tyre will come with a gift; men of wealth will seek your favor. All glorious is the princess within her chamber; her gown is interwoven with gold. In embroidered garments she is..." (Psalm 45 10-14).

Once when Kevin and I were in Paris we had the chance to go to the palace at Versailles, the incredible palace of King Louis the XVI. The palace was fabulous, the grounds amazing and the tour guides delightful. We were walking in the outer gardens on a tour when we heard the story of how the peasants, the common people of the day, went in to visit with the King. You see, you couldn't go into the King's presence without the proper clothes; therefore, at the edge of the palace grounds there would be clothes for rent, one simply had to exchange one's peasant clothes for the attire required at the palace and then you were allowed access to the King. How true for us as believers! We have a most wonderful King, the King of Kings and He requires we are dressed a certain way so that we might enter into His presence. We have seen our princess mourning, being glorious and now, she is getting dressed! No small task on one's wedding day.

My daughter is in my niece's wedding this month. My sister and I have made the two lovely little flower girl dresses. My sister added little beads and golden lace, an almost embroidered look, and I love it. The gowns have a Cinderella-like feel. Now we are finished and on the weekend the girls will dress up and be found to be beautiful, fit to be seen in the wedding; how much more so my niece. She will have her hair and her nails done and whatever else will make her ready for her wedding day. We may forget, at times, that we are a "bride being made ready." How are our alterations going? How is our gown? What are we dressed in? These are some of the questions I want to consider in this week's study. We are called to be dressed, are we not?

Read Isaiah 61:10-62:5

1. With what are we clothed and by whom?

God does not require us to find our own garments; He longs to clothe us in His righteousness. This is not of our own doing and we can only say on bended knee, "This is marvelous in our eyes." We have a gracious and mighty God, who not only loves us and longs for us to be His bride; He also provides our garments for us. I remember years ago, when Kevin and I were planning our wedding, I had absolutely no clue what I was doing but I knew three things: I needed to have a dress, I needed to have flowers and I needed to have a cake. That was it- I'm sure I needed one of those "Plan your wedding in 102 days" books, but I wasn't even wise enough to get a book! Needless to say, all these things were arranged; friends offered to make a cake (just as it should be in God's economy- exceedingly, abundantly beyond all I could ask or imagine!) and I picked out flowers one day (at the florist I just logically picked out practical, inexpensive flowers, being told what to do.) But the wedding dress, oh, I was at a loss. I wanted to be beautiful--surely I did--but I had no idea how to believe Kevin was enthralled with me (remember I had to, "forget my people and my father's house" and my father's words.) Then too, I really had no money with which to buy a lovely wedding dress, but Kevin did. Not only did my bridegroom provide the love and safety and security I needed to flourish in his love, he also provided my wedding dress. I remember the day we went to a bridal shop in Colorado with his Mom, we shopped and found a beautiful "puffed-sleeve" dress with all kinds of embroidery on it and Kevin's Mom cried and said I was beautiful. Kevin never saw the dress till our wedding day, but he paid for it; how much more so has the Bridegroom of Heaven, who laid down His life for us so that we might have garments of salvation. Our robes of righteousness cost Him His life, but He was willing to spill His blood to wash us clean, to make us righteous in His Father's sight, so that He might hold us by the hand, bringing us to the Father's heart and say, "Isn't she beautiful, Father, I told You You would love her at first sight." We are clothed with garments of salvation and robes of righteousness and brought to the King. We are His beloved child and He is well-pleased to give us to His Son.

Read Isaiah 61:1-3

2. What is this Son like, the One who has come to rescue us? What does He give us?

64

We find a captive in need of rescue, and a Savior comes to free her. She needs so much more than rescue: we find her mourning and she needs to be comforted. We find her in ashes (a sign of mourning) but she is given a crown of beauty. If we could exchange "a crown of beauty" for our ashes, the "oil of gladness" for our mourning, the "garment of praise" for our spirit of despair, we would be changed. Do not overlook the fact that we find ourselves in mourning and there is One who comes to comfort, to heal the broken-hearted. Do not overlook your own sorrows. God wants to take them and exchange them for joy, but first comes the mourning, the real heart-wrenching pain. Allow God access to whatever pain or hurt or disappointment you are carrying in your heart and you will find He comes to comfort and provide. What does the Lord provide for our mourning? He provides Himself. When we are ready, when we are done grieving, there will be a bigger space in our hearts for God. All that was filled with pain and longing has been broken open and is ready to receive Him. Yes, He gives us a crown of beauty. You are cherished- each day try to remember to look in the mirror and feel for the crown on your head. The Lord also gives us a garment of praise. A garment is something we choose to put on, though. What have you chosen? Have you chosen despair? Have you chosen to set that despair aside, to mourn and then to move into the loving arms of your Savior, who is holding a garment of praise for you? He has come to heal and restore.

Read Revelation 19:7-9; Ephesians 2:10

3. How can we, as the church, the Bride of Christ, make ourselves ready for Him?

As we consider how we are clothed and who clothes us we realize that our "wedding dress," the garment of salvation, is a gift from Christ and the fine linen is a reflection of what we have done in our lives, the "good works" we have been called to live out. It is not as though we can earn any kind of entrance to the palace of the King of Kings with our good works; it is only that if we are to be His bride and reflect His love, then how can we come to Him with empty hands and hearts? There is no conflict between the "garments of salvation" and the fine linen garments, which are the righteous acts of the saints. Salvation brings us to a Savior who has a wedding dress for us, and our Christian life is all about our linen garments, acts of mercy and good works that show the world God's love and bring His love to bear on unbearable circumstances. I am not talking about being a missionary or necessarily huge acts of Christian service, but I am wondering if it might be helpful for us to consider what we are living for. Are we living for "creature comforts" or are we living to serve our King? Are we at all concerned about the persecuted church or the homeless in the nearby city, or are we only wondering what we are to prepare for supper? These are hard questions to ask and answer, but if we are to be "dressed" in a way that pleases our Father it will require some alterations. James says it so succinctly: "Religion that God our Father accepts as pure and faultless is this: to look after orphans and widows in their distress and to keep oneself from being polluted by the world" (James 1:27). Later James writes: " Who is wise and understanding among you? Let him show it by his good life, by deeds done in the humility that comes from wisdom. But if you harbor bitter envy and selfish ambition in your hearts, do not boast about it or deny the truth. Such wisdom does not come down from heaven, but is earthly, unspiritual, of the devil. For where you have envy and selfish ambition, there you find disorder and every kind of evil practice. But the wisdom that comes from heaven is first of all pure, then peace-loving, considerate, submissive, full of mercy and good fruit, impartial and sincere. Peace-makers who sow in peace raise a harvest of righteousness" (James 3:13-18). These are very hard sayings, but it leads us into the idea of what is appropriate for us to "wear" as Christ's bride and what is not.

Read Colossians 3:5-17

4. What are we called to "put off" or rid ourselves of, and what are we called to "clothe ourselves with?"

Do you have any alterations that need to be made in your "dress" or life? I know I do. I cannot look at this list, or any others of Paul's for that matter, and not see things that I need to remove from my life. Look up Ephesians 4:22-32 if you'd like another view of the "put off/put on" responsibility of the Christian. How do these lists impact our lives? Can we say we have altered our character at all since we have come to know Christ? We have a "job" to do as followers of Christ, and that is to be growing more and more like Him and closer and closer to Him. Is this happening in your life? Are you finding that the closer you walk with God the more He shows you what could be removed from your life? It is both our privilege and great fear to submit ourselves to the Holy

Spirit and allow Him access to hearts. When we can "put off" old resentments, bitterness and rage over wrong-doings, our hearts are free to love. Love covers a multitude of sins, but we do not always want to love- we want to harbor the very qualities Paul challenges us to rid ourselves of. Listen to Jude's challenge: "But you, dear friends, build yourselves up in your most holy faith and pray in the Holy Spirit. Keep yourselves in God's love as you wait for the mercy of our Lord Jesus Christ to bring you to eternal life. Be merciful to those who doubt; snatch others from the fire and save them; to others show mercy, mixed with fear-hating even the clothing stained by corrupted flesh" (Jude 20-23). Jude gives us a wonderful way to live. We can be filled with mercy when we "keep ourselves in God's love". When we are aware of the incredible love God has for us and rest there, keep ourselves there, then we will find we are able to "put off" qualities and "put on" others. Our proximity to the Savior requires alterations in our character. We cannot come into the King's presence and remain there without the Holy Spirit prompting us, "Do you mind changing your clothes, this really isn't appropriate for the Lord's presence? Would you mind, terribly, taking that rag outside the palace, we don't allow that kind of clothing in here?" Keep yourselves in God's love. We are safe there, we are challenged there, and the Holy Spirit will cause us to look at the clothing we have on and say, "This is appropriate," or, "I need to make alterations." What are you wearing today - anything that needs to be altered? Ask the Holy Spirit, He is a most excellent Tailor of our characters.

Read Romans 13:14 and Galatians 3:27

5. Who are we clothed with?

When we accept Christ we are "clothed with Him." How does this work, really? Remember the verses in Isaiah? We are given robes of righteousness and when God looks at us He sees Christ. We are covered in the blood of the Lamb and made righteous before God. One way to grow in Christ is to ask ourselves this question: "If I am now clothed in Christ and wearing His robes of righteousness, is what I am doing now, or saying now or thinking now consistent with these robes?" If we had on a wedding gown we would want our under garments to be fitting as well. This takes us back to the "fine linen garments of the saints (which are their righteous acts.)" It is not enough to "look" like a Christian on the outside; one's inner life must match up. 1 Samuel 16: 7 says this: "The Lord does not look at the things man looks at. Man looks at the outward appearance, but the Lord looks at the heart." It is our hearts that we must be concerned with. "Your beauty should not come from outward adornment, such as braided hair and the wearing of gold jewelry and fine clothes. Instead, it should be that of your inner self, the unfading beauty of a gentle and quiet spirit, which is of great worth in God's sight. For this is the way the holy women of the past who put their hope in God used to make themselves beautiful" (1 Peter 3:3-5). This is a woman who has been in her "inner chamber" and has made herself ready. She is concerned about her beauty, yes, but it is the beauty of her heart that is most revealing. What are we most concerned about? Is it our outward appearance or the inner self?

Read Matthew 22:1-14

6. What is this parable about? Who are those who are "dressed" properly and who are those who are not?

Why is the King so severe in His demands about what kind of dress is allowed at the wedding? Why can't people just "come as they are" to the wedding, or as is the metaphor, into heaven? We need to consider our presumptuous attitude that at times can look something like this, "I can go as I want, and I don't have to dress up." Or, "Why were they invited? They aren't dressed right!" We can be so quick to let ourselves off the "hook" as far as attitudes, motives and internal sins go, and yet judge others so severely because we somehow don't think that *they* belong in church or in heaven. How many of us really feel that the thief on the cross belongs in heaven? Sure, he made a "death-bed" confession of faith, but what if the "death-bed confession of faith" came from a sexual offender or a murderer or someone who wounded you severely? Does our mercy go that far? If someone had been wearing "rags" (living a sinful life) all their lives and then they showed up at the wedding (heaven) and changed their clothes (accepted Christ's robes of righteousness and garments of salvation), would we want them there? Would we go out looking for those living in sin and say, "Here, this is the way, 'try on' Christ's love and see if that 'fits' you better than sin? You were made for clothes far grander than sin and shame – try on salvation, try on Christ's righteousness and see how that looks on you." We would do this perhaps for our friends and family that we dearly love because we long to give them the key to being "well-dressed" which is salvation; but would we extend the offer of "new clothes" to the forsaken, the homeless, those in our families that we hate? This is what Jude means when he says, "Be merciful to those who doubt; snatch others from the fire and save them; to others show mercy, mixed with fear- hating even the clothing stained by corrupted flesh" (verses 22, 23). It takes a great deal of mercy to "snatch people from the fire." To show mercy is to express the heart of Christ to a hurting world. If we are "clothed" in Christ then we are to be so like Him that if someone were to glance at you they would not be sure, was that Christ acting and living, or was it you? Do we live in a way, clothed in a way, which our Father in Heaven and our brothers and sisters on earth are seeing "Christ in you the hope of glory?" It is a high calling, but we are to be "perfect even as your Father in heaven is perfect." When the world looks at us and sees mercy and grace then we are a little closer to being "dressed" as the Lord would want us to be "dressed."

John Chrysostom writes this:

> "How did you come here not having a wedding garment? So here he does not mean a garment, but fornication, and foul and unclean living. As then foul garments signifies sin, so do golden garments signifies virtue. But this garment belonged to the King. He Himself bestowed the garment upon her: for she was naked and disfigured. He is not speaking of clothing, but of virtue. Observe: the expression itself has great nobility of meaning. He does not say 'in a garment of gold' but in a garment 'woven with gold'. Listen intelligently. A garment of gold is one that is gold throughout: but a garment woven with gold is one which is partly of gold and partly of silk." [1]

We have been given godly qualities that are interwoven with our humanity. We are not perfect, but we are called to weave God's love and mercy, His grace and forgiveness, His joy and faithfulness into the fabric of our lives. Then, as we live, a golden thread is woven throughout our life and we find we reflect more and more the nobility and grace of our calling as children of the King. Just as The Prince and the Pauper can change clothes and make the world believe they are someone else, so too, can we. We can so reflect the Father's love that the world is perplexed. We are God's own dear child and the world sees Him when they see us. We have become royalty as we change our clothes.

Read Revelation 3:1-6 and 3:14-21

7. What is the passage written to the church in Sardis referring to? How can one's clothes be "soiled?" How can we be "dressed in white?" What is written to the church in Laodicea? How have they been "naked?"

Are we ever, especially in our society, "clothed but naked?" Is there something we can do to clothe ourselves? What will it take for me realize I am not "dressed" as my Lord would have me be dressed and there is only one place I can go to get the right clothes? All the magazines and latest fashion statements will not cover up a heart that has no room for the lost. Nothing I can wear can cover up a bitter, angry heart. I can only go to my Father's lap and rest. I must be with Him; I must immerse myself in His love. I must *let* Him love me- I must keep myself in God's love, for out of that will flow my good deeds and righteous acts, my "fine linen garments." There is One who has come to give me a white robe and this same One has called me to "dress" myself in a way that would honor Him.

"Father God, You have created us and know exactly what "fits" each of us best. Help us to be willing to stand before You and allow ourselves to be "altered" by You and dressed in Your garments of salvation and robes of righteousness. We thank You and praise You for loving us so perfectly. Amen.

Chapter 6

Called to Be Led

"Listen, O daughter, consider and give ear: Forget your people and your father's house. The King is enthralled by your beauty; honor Him, for He is your Lord. The Daughter of Tyre will come with a gift; men of wealth will seek your favor. All glorious is the princess within her chamber; her gown is interwoven with gold. In embroidered garments she is led to the King; her virgin companions follow her and are brought to you..."

The wedding day has come for our beautiful bride; she is ready, all glorious, and now she is being led to the King. As we consider this study on being led by God, we need to consider what we expect from God when we ask Him to lead us. How will He lead us? Where will He lead us? What kind of path will He choose for us, and what will we be asked to "walk through"? These are all the questions we will examine as we look at our glorious princess being led.

Read Exodus 15:13

1. Where does God say He will lead His people and with what two qualities does He say He will lead them?

A few years ago my husband, Kevin, and I had an opportunity to take a dance lesson. It was just one night of dancing and the instructors were on hand to help you if you wanted to learn a new dance step or improve your dancing. The instructors circled the room, available at any time (I think they were on the hunt for their next victims!). Kevin and I surely caught their eye; we couldn't dance because I refused to be led! Oh, I blamed it all on Kevin! He didn't know how to lead; but as the dance instructors separated us, and the male instructor danced with me and Kevin with the female instructor it became very clear: I didn't want to be led. I didn't trust myself to my partner (even if he was a polished dance teacher). I didn't submit to his strong arms almost forcing me to the next step in the dance. I didn't like being "pushed around". That is what I thought being led felt like. Someone was pushing me into places I didn't want to go, and if they cared about me, I wouldn't be in a "hard place" experiencing "hard things" or suffering at all.

My misconceptions about dancing were only the tip of the iceberg compared to my misconceptions about being led as God's child. God says He leads us with unfailing love and leads us in His strength. He never says He will lead us to "easy" places or on "easy" paths, only that His love is unfailing and His strength no one can fathom. He is strong, and He is loving. These are the keys to walking the path God has led you on. If you can hold these truths in your heart--that no matter how high the mountain seems or how difficult the path looks, God is strong enough to carry you and His love is unfailing; His love will not, nay cannot fail you--then your heart will be led in peace, and you will find yourself in good strong arms, and your heart will dance with the One who placed you on your path.

Read Isaiah 43:15-21

2. To what historical event is this passage referring? (Read Exodus 14:19-31.) How did the Israelites respond to God's deliverance? (For further reading try the "song of the redeemed" in Exodus 15.) What are we to "forget"? Where does God "make a way"? What happens to the "wasteland"?

God has unusual paths for us to follow. Where we ever got the notion that we would have 'smooth sailing and calm seas' I'm not sure! God makes a way for us in the desert! I would like for Him to make a way for me through a lush garden. I think, after all, if He is the God of the universe, He could "arrange" things for me. I'm not asking for much, really, just a comfortable life with no sickness, and children who are happy and healthy and well-adjusted. All I want is for God to use me where I am, where I am comfortable and happy. Ouch! Isaiah seems to indicate that God leads us when we are in a desert (often times that translates to when we feel like we are in a desert). Life can be difficult, we know, but we are hoping that God is going to make it easier for us, that He will be kind of a "genie in a bottle" to help us. When our path seems difficult, we may feel that we might have done something wrong, or we pray for God to deliver us; but God says He makes a way **"in** the desert" not around it. Nothing we can do can short-circuit the path God has for us.

What is the one thing you crave if you are in the desert? Have you ever walked in a real desert, in the scorching heat of a desert like the Sonoran Desert? Our family hiked several years ago in California, and all we craved was refreshment. We needed shelter, we needed water, and we needed rest from the sun beating on us. The one thing we crave in our spiritual desert is refreshment. God tells us, "I will refresh the weary and satisfy the faint" (Jeremiah 31:25). We crave the Lord's presence in our lives and His real shelter. This is why God makes a way "*in* the desert" and not around it--so we will crave Him above all else. He wants us to want Him, and sometimes that means having us "need" Him. We face circumstances and situations that seem impossible to us— stretching out before our eyes seem days or weeks of suffering, or months and years of exhausting trials with our children, with our jobs or our spouses, and we don't know how we will make it, how we will "get through".

We will get through just as God says: we will grieve: "Forget the former things, do not dwell on the past" (Philippians 3:13). We will have hope and be able to open our eyes to new possibilities: "See, I am doing a new thing! Now it springs up, do you not perceive it?" (Isaiah 43:18, 19) We will trust and walk: "I am making a way in the desert and streams in the wasteland." If I had been willing to forget my fear of being led by someone else and had trusted myself to the dance instructor, I might have had one of the most glorious dances I had ever known, but I was unwilling to forget how I had always danced, protecting myself. I didn't want to trust another, yet how much more so to trust the "Dance Instructor" of my soul. He desires to dance with me and waltz with me. He wants to lead me with loving-kindness and in His strength. If you are in a hard place on the "dance floor of life", will you trust yourself to One who does new things and promises to provide for us and turn our wastelands into streams of living water? This is what He does for the soul who trusts in Him. If you are thirsty in the desert and needing refreshment, come to the One who says, "Come, all you who are thirsty, come to the waters... Give ear and come to Me that your soul may live" (Isaiah 55: 1, 3).

Read Jeremiah 31:1-5

3. With what has God "drawn us" to Him? Where will God lead us? What will we be like? (See verse 12.) What will God give us?

This picture, in Jeremiah, is a picture of God restoring and refreshing, "doing a new thing" with the clans of Israel. God's people had forsaken Him, followed after other gods and so they had gone off into captivity and suffered. God then says to them: "The people who survive the sword will find favor in the desert; I will come and give rest to Israel." How interesting is that? The people, we find out in verse 5, will plant vineyards and all, but more particular than that is the expression; "they will find favor in the desert." We often feel we have done something wrong or deserved our suffering in the desert places, but here God tells us we will find favor there. God says, "I have loved you with an everlasting love; I have drawn you with loving kindness." There is no sense of, "when you get out of the difficult place you are in then I will show you favor". God comes to give us rest *in* our desert places. He says, "I will come and give rest to Israel."

Do you wait in the desert for God to come to you? I do not. So often I am running, and the hotter the desert (translate, "the harder the trial"), the faster I am running from God. I feel forsaken, a little like Sarai's maid, the one who was cast out of Sarai and Abram's home in Genesis 16:6-13, "Sarai mistreated Hagar; so she fled from her. The angel of the Lord found Hagar near a spring in the desert; it was the spring that is beside the road to Shur. And he said, 'Hagar, servant of Sarai, where have you come from and where are you going?' 'I'm running away from my mistress Sarai,' she answered. Then the angel of the Lord said, 'Go back to your mistress and submit to her.' And then the angel added, 'I will so increase your descendants that they will be too numerous to count.' This is the name that Hagar gave to the Lord who spoke to her: 'You are the God who sees me,' for she said, 'I have now seen the One who sees me.'"

Sometimes our "mistress" is suffering, and we run from her. Sometimes suffering comes into our lives; we can try to run from it, or we can choose to rest in the strong and loving God who promises to lead us and be with us. Perhaps the pain in our lives will open up places in our hearts that weren't open before. Or maybe in our pain and suffering, we realize we need God and can't make it on our own. We need to see Him and to know that He sees us and knows where we are. God can come and find us in the desert, like He did the handmaid of Sarai, and He will come to us, He says, and give us rest. Not all of our suffering is just or reasonable. Was it right for Sarai to mistreat Hagar because she was jealous? No, yet God could have "cut short" Hagar's suffering and He did not. God could have told Hagar to "move on" and find a "nicer" mistress, but He did not. God's path for us is the path to Him. God's goal for us is to bring us to Himself, to have us glimpse Him in all His glory in our lives—even in our deserts. God did not find Hagar in comfort, He found her in the desert. Is there some kind of desert in your heart or life right now? Are you lacking friendship or fellowship? Are you suffering under the weight of another diagnosis or another disappointment regarding your children or the children you do not yet have? This is your desert, and God sees you. He has not forsaken you; He has actually engraved you in the palm of His hand. (See Isaiah 49:15, 16.)

Read Isaiah 49:9-16

4. God's compassion is so evident to these captives. What does God offer them in the desert? Who guides these captives, and where does he lead them?

Comfort and compassion is God's compass. He leads us with these aspects of Himself just as we lead ourselves through an orienteering exercise with a real compass. God knows no other way. Even though we feel forsaken and persecuted, we are assured of God's comfort and compassion. No mountain is thrown into the sea in Isaiah, though; instead, the mountain becomes a road. I have seen this happen up in the mountains of Waterville Valley, where tiny little mountains are turned into roads to make the area more accessible. Projects like this take tons of drilling and lots of blasting material and hard labor. Is our heart so very different from that? God has to drill into us the lessons He has for us. Sometimes God has to "blast away" all our security or comfort. The effort it takes for us to hang on and have hope and trust God in this whole process is the "hard labor" required to turn the mountain we are facing into a road we can travel on. God's path always leads to a stream, a stream of living water which always awaits us as we journey on our spiritual path. We find that He has come to lead us to streams of refreshment.

God deals so tenderly with us, although we can perceive Him to be harsh or severe. Listen to Hosea's words in Hosea 11:1-4. "When Israel was a child I loved him, and out of Egypt I called my son. But the more I called Israel, the further they went from Me.... It was I who taught Ephraim to walk, taking them by the arms; but they did not realize it was I who healed them. I led them with cords of human kindness, with ties of love; I lifted the yoke from their neck and bent down to feed them." God has specifically led us with ties of love, even though we do not recognize it at times.

Consider John Chrysostom's words:

> "For this reason the devil plunges us into
> thoughts of despair so that he might cut us
> off from the hope which is towards God,
> the safe anchor, the foundation of our life,
> the guide of the way which leads to
> heaven, the salvation of perishing souls.
> 'For by hope,' it is said, 'we are saved'.
> For this is assuredly like some strong cord,
> suspended from the heavens, which
> supports our souls and gradually draws us
> towards that world on high, we are to cling
> to this firmly and be lifted up above the
> tempest of life."[1]

Let us be clinging, like a life-line, all the way to heaven, by faith and hope, and hold on for dear life to the anchor of our souls until we "make it to the other side."

Read Jeremiah 31:9-14 and Revelation 7:17

5. Where, again, does God say He will lead us? In Revelation, what will He do for us? What will mourning be turned into? How about sorrow? Do we see a repeat of the process of grieving and being comforted by our God?

We find the whole scene here in Jeremiah breath-taking. God says His people will come with weeping and they will pray as He brings them back from captivity. God tenderly leads them beside streams of living water. I wonder where we are on our journey towards God and His streams of living water. Perhaps we are weeping, still mourning. Or perhaps we have already joined the maidens in their dance. Wherever we are, God has promised to gather us and to be a shepherd to us. This is where we find our garden. It is no wonder our hearts long for shelter and a garden--we were made for glorious places and our hearts long for Eden. We are here, in the scorching heat of our desert; yet each day God calls to us and says, "I am here, I will comfort you, I will lead you to streams of living water, I will wipe away your tears." For every circumstance and situation we cannot understand God says, "I will come to you there; there in your pain and suffering I will meet you."

There is a garden in the midst of your soul where God longs to water you and fill you. He longs to make a garden of you, that He might lead others to Himself by the fragrant offering of your heart. 2 Corinthians 2:14-15 reads as follows: "But thanks be to God, who always leads us in triumphal procession in Christ and spreads everywhere the fragrance of the knowledge of Him. For we are to God the aroma of Christ among those who are being saved and those who are perishing." We must spread the knowledge of God, but we cannot spread what we do not know. If we are like Hagar, running in the desert from suffering, then we must stop long enough to see that God sees us and to know, in our very hearts, that God will meet us there. If we are not suffering, we cannot give false comfort and pious answers to those sitting in the scorching heat. Surely, God will not give us more than we can handle, as we sometimes say, but what He gives us is Himself. If we have not learned that, we cannot share it. God's goal in leading is always to lead us to Himself, to fill us with Himself. He knows what we need to need Him.

Read Psalm 27:11; Psalm 142:1-3; Psalm 143:8-10

6. What kind of path do we want? Who leads us?

I want a level path, a smooth road, an easy life. I don't want to suffer, and I really don't want to learn any hard lesson. I also beg God to not let my children suffer. If my life were up to me, I would ask for comfort and security. Instead, God gives me Himself. I am promised that He is "Immanuel, God with us." What keeps me going when I'm challenged is knowing that there is a God who knows me and sees me and walks with me. I can look at circumstances as unbearable, or I can come to God and say, "God, I can't bear this, I can't go on in this situation, but You see me and You know me and I know You are with me." It is my crying out that saves me; when I try to live from my own strength or my own ideas I do not always fare so well. My challenge is to turn my heart and mind upward and seek God. The goal for us is to be led by God and to God. Whatever happens in our lives, God will use and redeem and restore, that we might know Him and love Him. He is after our hearts and He longs to draw us to Himself. We know that "All things work together for good for those who love Him and are called according to His purpose" (Romans 8:28). God's design is to call us and justify us and glorify us by making us like His Son, and, lest we forget, His Son suffered. Peter reminds us, "Do not be surprised at the painful trial you are suffering, as though something strange were happening to you. But rejoice that you participate in the sufferings of Christ, so that you may be overjoyed when His glory is revealed" (1 Peter 4:12, 13).

We are called to the path that will take us to God. For some it is an easy, though narrow road; for others, the road is fraught with trials and suffering that the faint of heart could not stand. We can't know God's economy of suffering (read Job 19:7, 8), but we can know His heart. His heart is always one of love towards us and faithfulness. "His ways are higher than our ways and His thoughts are higher than our thoughts" (Isaiah 55: 8, 9). As Job says, "He knows the way I take and when He has tested me, I shall come forth as gold" (Job 23:10). God always knows the ways we take. Consider Proverbs 16:9: "In his heart a man plans his course, but the Lord determines his steps." God leads us places we might not have planned on going, but He knows the way we take. He determines our steps, and if we can remember that He always leads us in loving-kindness and faithfulness, our hearts will be filled with peace.

Read Psalm 139:23, 24; Psalm 61:2-4

7. What guides us? Where are we led?

God longs to lead us in the way everlasting. He wants to refresh us when we are weary and strengthen us when we are faint. It is as if there is an oasis in the desert, and every morning God says, "My mercies are new every morning, come and be refreshed before you begin your day. It's going to be a scorcher out there; have you had enough time with Me to 'face the heat'?" All these questions from the heart of a God who knows the way we take. He is not surprised when our children disappoint us; He is not alarmed with the test results from the doctor. He knows already the path we take. Allow yourself to trust that the heart of God is good toward you, that you can trust Him to lead you on this dance of life. We may not like the first step because it could be one of mourning as we let go of the way we have always danced-- independently, with self-sufficiency and alarming ease. Now, Someone wants to take our hand and lead us--and He will lead us to some wonderful places, but also some very difficult ones. There will be mountains in our way, and we will pray. Sometimes they will be moved; sometimes they will be made into a road. Trust the Architect of the Highway. There is one Way to the Father, and that is the way God leads us. Are you coming? The way is often steep and the road sometimes long, but find good traveling companions and journey on--on to the heart of God.

"God, please lead us. We want to ask that You will lead us on level ground, that our feet will not stumble, that we won't fall, but, God, You alone know our hearts. Lead us however you will, as long as You lead us Home to You. In Christ's Name we pray, Amen."

Chapter 7

Called to Joy

"Listen, O daughter, consider and give ear: Forget your people and your father's house. The King is enthralled by your beauty; honor Him, for He is your Lord. The daughter of Tyre will come with a gift; men of wealth will seek your favor. All glorious is the princess within her chamber; her gown is interwoven with gold. In embroidered garments she is led to the King; her virgin companions follow her and are brought to you. They are led in with joy and gladness" (Psalm 45: 10-15).

Here is our beautiful bride being led to the King and she is joyful. She is led with joy and gladness. As we consider this part of the study on being led with joy, I wonder what our expectations are. Are we asking God to give us joy? Do we want to be happy? Are joy and happiness the same thing? What is our source of joy and how does joy manifest itself in our lives? These are all things to ponder as we look at our princess being "led in with joy and gladness."

Read Deuteronomy 16:13-15, 1 Chronicles 29:22

1. What circumstances caused the Israelites to be joyful? Where do we find joy?

We were at a recent family wedding I shocked some of my siblings because I was dancing! Now, if you were at a wedding and the bride and all her attendants were dancing, wouldn't it make you want to jump on your feet and dance? In the midst of all the celebration and the joyous occasion there was every reason to dance. Being with the bride and basking in her joy was cause enough for me to be joyful, and how much more so when I am in the presence of God. Psalm 43:3, 4 says this, "Send forth your light and your truth, let them guide me; let them bring me to your holy mountain, to the place where you dwell. Then will I go to the altar of God, to God, my joy and my delight. I will praise you with the harp, O God, my God." When we allow God to lead us to Himself amidst all that is happening in our lives, we find we are led to our joy, which is God Himself. When God becomes our joy and delight our hearts are at peace and we find we can face things- good or bad- that we weren't sure we could endure before.

If we allow God to replace all the "happiness" we are craving in our lives, a deep peace settles in on us that cannot be removed. In our culture of instant gratification and self-serving happiness it is hard to imagine being joyful just being in God's presence. There is something in us and in the messages which our culture sends to us which make things harder than that. We say to ourselves, "I'll be happy when the kids are in school," or, "I'll be happy when my husband's job settles down or he pays more attention to me." "I'll be happy when my kids are out of the teenage years." "I'll be happy when my kids are grown and settled." "I would be happy if I had my kids back at home, or if my marriage were going better." "I would be happy if I were married, or if I was married to someone else!" Our culture screams for us to figure out what would make us happy- a better weight or a better mate, obedient children or attentive husbands.

What does it take to make us happy? We want our circumstances arranged, in order, to our liking. Wherever we are we find we can add, "I'll be happy when…." (fill in your own blank). If we are home we say, "I'll be happy when we go away." If we are away we say, "I'll be happy when we are home again." Our happiness need not be circumstantial. We find that the Israelites were happy in one place when they were in the presence of God. Their limitations need not haunt us, though. The Israelites were a joyful people when they were in God's house praising their God, but if they were in exile, you couldn't drag a song out of them. (See Psalm 137:1-6) At times, our hearts and souls are "captive" and cannot be joyful because we are bound by unseen captors. Sometimes, things in our lives hold us in captivity and we are not always aware of them- it may be past sin, not forgiving someone, or unresolved anger. Some of these issues will not be resolved by simply deciding to be joyful. If you find yourself like the Israelites unable to be joyful, ask God to show you what might be in your heart holding you back (keeping you captive) and ask Him to be your Healer. Always, though, seek the help of a professional counselor or trusted friend if what you find in your heart overwhelms you.

The people of God were joyful when they were praising God in His sanctuary. We have no such need because we do not need to be in God's sanctuary to be praising Him although it does help. We can praise Him and be joyful at any time because He is always with us. We can be in the worst of situations and He is there, leading us and guiding us and wanting to be our light. He desires to be our light and our delight. What stops us from truly trusting God and abiding in Him in a way that fulfills us? We want so much to be fulfilled and find joy in what we do. God clearly says, though, that He is our light and salvation. He is the One who made us and He is also the source of our joy. We are called to joy, but the source of that joy is beyond us. The source of joy is in God Himself.

Listen to what Augustine has to say regarding this:

> "And your people will rejoice in You." To their own evil they will rejoice in themselves: to their own good they will rejoice in You. For when they wished to have joy of themselves, they found in themselves woe: but now because God is all our joy, he that will rejoice securely, let him rejoice in Him who cannot perish. For why, my brothers, will you rejoice in silver? Either your silver perishes, or you: and no one knows which first: yet this is certain, that both shall perish. For neither can man remain here always nor can silver remain here always: so too gold, so garments, so houses, so money, so broad lands, so lastly, this light itself. Be not willing then to rejoice in these: but rejoice in that light which has no setting: rejoice in that dawn which no yesterday precedes, which no tomorrow follows. What light is that? 'I,' says He, 'am the light of the world.' He who says, 'I am the light of the world,' calls you to Himself. When He calls you He converts you; when He converts you, He heals you; when He heals

you, you will see your Converter, unto whom it is said, 'Show us Your mercy, O Lord, and grant us Your salvation'; Your salvation, which is Christ. Happy is he unto whom God shows His mercy. He cannot indulge in pride, because God showed him mercy. For by showing him His salvation He persuades him that whatever good man has, he has only from Him who is all our good. And when a man has seen that whatever good man has is not from himself, but from his God; he sees that everything which is praised in him is of the mercy of God, not of his own deserving; and seeing this, he is not proud; and not being proud he is not lifted up; not being lifted up he does not fall; not falling, he stands; standing, he clings fast; clinging fast, he abides; abiding, he enjoys, and rejoices in the Lord his God. He who made him shall be to him a delight; and his delight no one shall spoil, no one interrupts this delight, no one takes it away."[1]

When we cling to God and abide in Him there is no fear that our joy will be taken away. We are sure that God is faithful and true; we have come to know that we are His delight and now we delight in Him also. Joy is in the relationship we have with God and in the perspective it brings on our life. "If God is for us who can be against us?" Paul asks us in Romans 8:31. Psalm 56:9b- 13 says, "God is for me. In God whose word I praise, in the Lord, whose word I praise- in God I trust, I will not be afraid. What can man do to me? I am under vows to You, O God; I will present my thank offerings to You. For You have delivered me from death and my feet from stumbling, that I may walk before God in the light of life." God has a path for us and it leads straight to Him. He is to be our joy and our salvation. The key for us is to "stand and cling and abide and enjoy" the Lord. The Westminster Confession says that the chief end of man is to "know and enjoy God forever." Have we ever considered this as our highest goal? I am afraid I rarely think of enjoying God. I want to please Him and serve Him and be obedient, but there is an aspect of enjoying that makes me uncomfortable. I am like the Israelites who had rules and regulations reminding them that they were to worship God and enjoy Him at certain times during certain festivals and at certain places.

Read John 4:4-24

2. How does Jesus say we worship?

Jesus gives us a whole new freedom to enjoy Him. There is no location now that is required as it was in the Jewish tradition. We can worship God in our spirits and find true joy there, just as the Jews found true joy in the House of God. Taking the time, though, to center our hearts on the Living God is a challenge. We want to "live our own lives and make our own way." We do not really want to need God and so we find ourselves digging wells and cisterns that are leak and break. Jeremiah 2:13 says, "My people have committed two sins: they have forsaken Me, the spring of living water, and have dug their own cisterns, broken cisterns that cannot hold water." A cistern is meant to hold water that refreshes and sustains life, but God tells us that the cisterns that we dig are broken in their very nature. God offers us Himself, a spring of living water, yet we sometimes choose a broken cistern instead. Many things we go to don't fulfill us and bring us life. Wealth, power, prestige, popularity, fame, health, and youth- all these appeal to our senses. We are drawn to explore some kind of magical way to fix whatever is wrong with our joy. If we are getting older we try anti-aging cream, if we are getting heavier we try a new diet, if our children aren't behaving we try a new parenting book, if we aren't behaving we try a self-help book! We look on our own for wisdom that will refresh us, for water that will quench the thirst that we have for meaning. Jesus offered a thirsty, worn-out woman the gift of eternal life and joy when He said, "Whoever drinks of the water I give him will never thirst. Indeed, the water I give him will become a spring of water welling up to eternal life" (John 4:14). Jesus has something to offer that we can find nowhere else: ever-lasting refreshment, the true satisfaction of eternal life. All we crave in this life is found in one place. Meaning, purpose, significance, joy and life: all these are found at the fountain at His feet. The question for us remains: where will we look for joy? If we are relying on our circumstances to dictate joy, then we will never know lasting and true joy.

Read Nehemiah 2:3; 4:7-9

3. What is causing Nehemiah grief?

All was not right with Nehemiah's world. He was an Israelite with a "cushy job" in the King's palace, but he had news of the Israelites in Jerusalem that upset him: the walls of God's city were broken down. Ezra, the priest, had reconstructed the temple of God, but the city itself lay in ruins. (If you have time to read Nehemiah chapters 1-8; it gives a rich history of grief and joy, struggle and triumph.) So Nehemiah leaves a comfortable position where he has been serving God, and goes to help the people of God rebuild the walls of His city. This call is not something I would embrace, but sometimes God takes us to places we would rather not go. Nehemiah wept and grieved and mourned over God's city and its people and then he went to make a difference. Perhaps we assume things will go smoothly for Nehemiah and God's people; after all, Nehemiah has been obedient, his heart has grieved and been stirred to rebuild the walls of this ancient city, but we find Nehemiah is beset with great opposition. I would want God to "smooth the path before me," but that doesn't happen. Sometimes my expectation is that because I am serving God things will be easy, but that is not the case for Nehemiah. When we grieve our losses, we must articulate them and live through them with the grace of God to help.

Nehemiah just pours everything out to God. In my life, that prayer or grief looks something like this: "God, what am I to do? My life and my children's lives are filled with such a lack of regard for You. What am I to do when I feel that my children are disobedient or I am too busy to even notice if they are disobedient? We are pushed and pulled along in the current of the culture and the 'walls and gates of our lives are in ruins'." I know it seems like an exaggeration, but did you ever think of our society's demands on us to "do it all and have it all" are like some kind of enemy seeking to destroy what God wants for our families? Maybe I've been in the trenches too long, but I've had a week like Nehemiah and the Israelites must have had; you see, even as they were building the walls of God's Holy City, the enemies were harassing them. Doing God's work does not exempt us from exhaustion and real enemies! So what did Nehemiah do? We find that Nehemiah is a man of prayer; first he prays and then he posts a guard, so that literally while one group of people are building the wall, the others are standing guard with their weapons. I think I might have sat down and cried and told God how hard it was to build a wall anyway and why didn't He come and protect me while I was working on His wall? That is how I felt this week as I lived my life and considered joy. I forgot to "stand and cling and abide and rejoice."

Read Nehemiah 8:10, Deuteronomy 16:15, Psalm 28:7-9

4. What was the source of strength for Nehemiah and his fellow Israelites? Where can we find strength?

Nehemiah was an amazing historian. There was no "revisionist" history with him; he told it like it was. I am struck again how we find a man of God who was the cup-bearer to King Artaxerxes, grieving. If we haven't learned this yet in our study we need to take note again: God's people grieve. After Nehemiah and the Israelites rebuild the city walls, they listened to God's word and were grieved for all the ways they had not obeyed the Lord. Has this ever happened to you? You have been busy for God, and yet sometimes in the midst of our working for God we lose sight of the fact that we are not obeying God. When we do open God's Word we are grieved at our own disregard for God's ways and for the sin on our lives. Here is where we find Nehemiah, and yet God graciously says to His people, through Nehemiah, "Do not be grieved, for the joy of the Lord is your strength. " God's ways, God's Law and His presence with us in our grieving are our strength. Be assured that when you come to God in repentance and mourning acknowledging your disobedience and neglect of God and His ways, He will restore you with His joy.

Read Zephaniah 3:17

5. What anchors me when I feel I am all alone and needing help?

Zephaniah reminds me that God is with me. I am helped, I am saved; there is a God who longs to come to me amidst all my chaos and sing over me. One afternoon recently, my thoughts were filled with how overwhelmingly complicated my life seemed to be: I was starting to get a cold, we had four soccer games, one dance class, one choir practice, two cross-country meets, one birthday party, one evening meeting for Daddy, one school meeting, one PSAT, a yard to rake and mow and laundry to fold! Never mind that the soccer socks were lost in the unfolded laundry, we couldn't find the dance shoes, one person needed new soccer cleats because they had grown so much in the last month and we lost the soccer shin guards! All these things harass me like some kind of invisible enemy. Instead of "standing guard" with my weapons of warfare, (see Ephesians 6:18) I found myself, not grieving my situation, but angry that God didn't make it easier. I wanted God to come and take all the enemies away; sometimes He does that, but sometimes He asks us to stand. Remember what

Augustine said, "stand and cling and abide and rejoice."
If I am not standing where am I? The call of the Christian
life is to live our lives in dependence on God and His
strength. As Nehemiah shows us, first we must grieve
over our situation (God, I don't have the strength for what
you are asking, I see what needs to be done in my family
or in your church, or in my relationships I see walls
broken down in my relationships, but I am too self
absorbed to care and I am too weak and there are too
many enemies and I only have my eyes on myself and my
limited ability) then St. Augustine's call to stand and cling
and abides challenges me.

Read Ephesians 6:10-14

6. What does Paul call us to do?

These scriptures are filled with "standing". When
we can stand, as Augustine calls us to do, we find we are
held in safe, strong arms. "The eternal God is our refuge
and underneath are the everlasting arms" (Deuteronomy
33:27). Standing requires trust. When I am tired or
"afraid in my tummy," as my little ones say, the last place
you will find me is standing. Generally you can find me
wallowing, saying "why is this happening to me? I can't
do "it" anymore or I can't 'take it' anymore." If I'm not
wallowing, I am whining: "God, why don't you help me,
can't you see I'm not strong enough for what you have
called me to do?" If I'm not wallowing or whining then
I'm in bed! "See, God, I give up! I'm tired and worn out
and I don't know where to find Your joy." God waits
patiently for me to stand. Standing means I go in His
strength to do the job He has given me, and "the joy of the

Lord is my strength" because I am standing in Him. I admit I can't do anything on my own (I'm not proud now, therefore I can't fall and can now stand) and I beg for His mercy to cover me and sustain me. Not many of us want to live here in this place of rest and trust and dependence; we are in the trenches with the Israelites begging God to protect us and His work as well. After we "stand" then we "cling" I consider prayer the "clinging part of Augustine's remarks. When we stand we are upright in God's presence and assured of His working on our behalf- we are aware of our enemies, aware of all the pitfalls that could overtake us, but we are engaged in life in a way that is making "Kingdom difference." When we "cling" we pray. Ephesians 6:18-20 is a call to pray. We are asked to pray five times in three verses! We are called to "pray in the spirit on all occasions with all kinds of prayers and requests… be alert and always keep on praying for all the saints." Prayer keeps us in a posture of clinging to God.

Read Isaiah 55:12; Psalm 16:11

7. What is our source of joy?

Joy is bigger than our own lives. When we need strength we are told, "The joy of the Lord will be our strength" (Nehemiah 8:10). What is the joy of the Lord? Could it be that God delights in all creation praising Him, in the whole earth being filled with His glory, in fellow believers lifting one another up, in walls being rebuilt, in the hungry being fed, in His word being spread? There is a sense of timelessness in the things of God: one cup of cold water given to a child in Christ's Name brings joy to the heart of God. Joy in my life means aligning my heart with the things that please the heart of God, binding up the broken hearted, setting captives free, rebuilding broken walls and lives; these things matter to God. God might not be so concerned with all my activities and which race is won and which college a child is attending *if* I am not feeding the hungry or clothing the naked.

The call to live in God's joy means God's joy is my strength. Is God's joy about my life as I choose to live it or about His purposes in my life? If I go to the soccer games, cross-country races, dance classes, choir practices and have not prayed or abided in God so that I am weary and overwhelmed and exhausted, I have been "digging and drinking from my own broken cistern." But if I serve God by living in a way that His life and His Spirit flow through me, no matter what I am called to do, then I am abiding. I had a favorite tree growing up that I would "abide" in. It wasn't a tree fort, it was just a tree I would climb from which I could watch the world. I need to climb into my Father's lap and gain that kind of perspective; I need to "abide" long enough in His presence and in prayer so that the way I perceived my world changes. I can stand and cling and abide long enough to know that God uses me in the little things, in the big things, in conversations and in playing with my children, on big trips and on little errands. All these can add up to days spent living from the source of joy- God Himself. There, in God's presence, is the place Augustine refers to when he says, "In abiding he enjoys and rejoices in the Lord his God."

"God, would you fill us with joy? Would you teach us to stand and cling and abide and rejoice in you? We want our lives to reflect your joy and to be led to you in joy."

Chapter 8

Called to Enter the King's Chambers

"Listen, O daughter, consider and give ear: Forget your people and your father's house. The King is enthralled by your beauty; honor Him, for He is your Lord. The Daughter of Tyre will come with a gift; men of wealth will seek your favor. All glorious is the princess within her chamber; her gown is interwoven with gold. In embroidered garments she is led to the King; her virgin companions follow her and are brought to you. They are led in with joy and gladness; they enter the palace of the King" (Psalm 45:10-15).

Once when I was in Munich, Germany I visited the palace in the city. It was a huge building with all kinds of modern uses, but one could still enter the place where the Kings had lived. I walked around the building for what seemed hours, I could not find the entrance! I found the museum, the beautiful gardens, the chapel, the café, but not the entrance to the palace. I eventually discovered the right door and was amazed by all the treasures and by the living quarters of the royalty. This is such a picture for me of how I sometimes view and live my life as a believer: I have been given access to the King of Kings but I wander around looking for a place to "fit in," perhaps wandering in the gardens or attending the chapel, or refreshing myself at the café, but rarely do I go running, led with joy and gladness, into the King's chambers. There is an intimacy and sense of purpose and longing that I lack. I am unsure I belong. I want to say that I have an intimate relationship with the King, but the reality in my life is I am very self-sufficient and I like to wander around the palace rather than spend my time in the King's chambers. What about you? Have you found your heart more comfortable seeking knowledge of your King (perhaps I could find you in the palace library) but not necessarily seeking *Him*. What is it that holds us back from all that God longs to give us in His presence? Joy and comfort, peace and purpose, unconditional love and kindness await us there. Will you join me as we journey into the King's presence this week?

Read Psalm 29:1-4, 9-11

1. How are we to worship the Lord? What strikes you about the power of the voice Lord in this Psalm? What does God say He will give His people?

I am humbled when I consider that the Lord sits enthroned over all the earth and everyone in His temple cries, "Glory!" Do I even begin to fathom how great a God we serve? I am afraid I need my perspective altered as I consider approaching Him. He is so much more holy and awesome than my mind can conceive, yet what strikes me is what God's voice can do! The voice of the Lord breaks Cedars and strips the forest bare! Just look out on a New England November day and you will see evidence of the power of the Lord's voice. More amazing to me than the power of the voice of the Lord is the tenderness with which that same voice speaks to me. I am reminded of the Lord's cry in Isaiah 40:1-5 "Comfort, comfort my people," says your God. "Speak tenderly to Jerusalem, and proclaim to her that her hard service has been completed, that her sin has been paid for, and that she has received from the Lord's hand double for all her sins. A voice of one calling: "In the desert prepare the way for the Lord; make straight in the wilderness a highway for our God. Every valley shall be raised up and every mountain and hill made low; the rough ground shall become level, the rugged places a plain. And the glory of the Lord will be revealed, and all mankind together shall see it." Two things happen in my life when the Lord speaks: I receive comfort and I see His glory.

I can arrange my heart and life so that I can hear the voice of the Lord. For some of us this takes more discipline than others, but you must know yourself. I need a quiet, clean place to hear what God has to say to me. Some people can sit in a favorite chair amidst chaos and hear God's voice -- how I envy you! I need a place where visual and auditory distractions are at a minimum; I'm not sure what I'm doing living in a house with five children! When I speak of hearing God's voice, to me that is a posture of listening. I can hear God "speak" by opening His word and reading. I can hear God "speak" by being quiet and reflecting on all His goodness to me. I can also hear God "speak" as I watch the forests being stripped bare! I ask God to help me listen. I ask Him what He wants me to hear and what I hear is His comfort, love and assurance; when I take the time to quiet myself His words to me are quiet songs of love for me. Remember Zephaniah 3:17?

Read Psalm 5:1-8, 11, 12

1. Who do we cry to for help? Who can dwell with God? What allows us to come into God's house?

We approach God with humility because of His greatness and yet we can appeal to His great mercy and compassion. "But I, by your great mercy have come into your house." I appreciate the way Eugene Peterson has translated this portion of scripture in *The Message Translation:* "And here I am –your invited guest- it's incredible. I enter your house; here I am prostrate in your inner sanctum. Waiting for directions… You'll welcome us with open arms when we run for cover to You. Let the party last all night! Stand guard over our celebration. You are famous God, for welcoming God-seekers, for decking us out in delight." I am God's guest. Have you ever thought of your Christian life that way? You are God's guest, He has been pleased to give you His Kingdom, and all that is required is true faith and humility. My refuge and my place of belonging is where He is. I can be glad in Gods' presence because He is glad to see me! What a thought, "What is man that you are mindful of him?" My assurance of God's delight in me is confirmed again in *The Message Translation*: "You are famous God, for welcoming God-seekers, for decking us out in delight." Do you find yourself there, in His presence and seeking His face? It's not a bad place to start the day- in the palace of the King.

Read Psalm 100:1-5, Jeremiah 10:7-13

3. What kind of qualities of the Lord are expressed here? Who are we in relationship to God? What are we called to do?

When I can be very clear about God, about who He is and who I am in relationship to Him, my life is ordered in a way that pleases Him. The key to living a joyful obedient Christian life is submission. If I can submit to the knowledge of God's Lordship and ownership of me, my whole life becomes centered on this: "Know that the Lord is God. It is He who made us, and we are His; we are His people and the sheep of His pasture." I can breathe here, I can rest here, and I can be loved here. In this knowledge of whose I am there is great freedom. I can grieve over what I have or do not have because I know I am held; I am His. God holds me in the palm of His hand and in this place of submission to His ownership of me, I can rest. This strong and mighty God is my God. I am His and He is mine and His banner over me is love. He claims me as His own by the very fact that He made me for His glory. Isaiah 43 reminds us of this: "But now, this is what the Lord says- He who created you, O Jacob, He who formed you, O Israel: 'Fear not, for I have redeemed you; I have summoned you by name; you are mine. When you pass through the waters, I will be with you; and when you pass through the rivers, they will not sweep over you. When you walk through the fire, you will not be burned; the flames will not set you ablaze. For I am the Lord, Your God, the Holy One of Israel, Your Savior... Since you are precious and honored in my sight, and because I love you, I will give men in exchange for you, and people in exchange for your life.... Bring my sons from afar and my daughter s from the ends of the earth- everyone who is called by My name, Whom I created for My glory, whom I formed and made." When I can listen for God's voice summoning me, even when I am going through very difficult times, I begin to have a sense of peace and purpose, direction and even delight. God longs for me to hear His words: "You are precious and honored in my sight, I've called you by name." Do you hear the call to intimacy? God longs to hold us as His precious child. Listen for His longing for you.

Read Hebrews 10:19-25

4. We are called into this relationship with the Father. What is the One way we are allowed access to the Father?

The Way to the Father requires an escort. Jesus says of Himself, "I am the way, the truth and the life. No one comes to the Father except through Me" (John 14:6). We are allowed entrance to the Holy of Holies, the Old Testament picture of intimacy with God, by the blood of the Lamb. There is a requirement of holiness that we cannot meet, no matter how we might long to be close to God. We must come through "the gate" and "the narrow road;" only Christ can escort us to His Father. Hebrews 9:24 tells us "Christ did not enter a man-made sanctuary that was only a copy of the true one; He entered heaven itself, now to appear for us in God's presence." Picture the Father calling our names, summoning us, as Isaiah says; we come to the entrance of the palace, but we are not allowed in. God longs to see us, but remember we don't have the right clothes. We need "garments of salvation," but all our righteous deeds, all those things we do that we think will make us special, are like filthy rags to God. We stand in the doorway, longing to go into the palace, longing to rush into God's presence with our companions, but sin will lock the door on us. Once we have acknowledged the work of Christ on the cross, then we are welcomed in through the way that Christ Himself has made for us. Christ appears for us in God's presence; He prepares the way for us to go to the Father! With Christ for us, nothing can separate us from the love of God which is in Christ Jesus our Lord, but to receive that love we must be "in Christ," wearing His robes of righteousness and clothed in His garments of salvation. If you have "the garments of salvation and the robes of righteousness" and still find yourself unable or unwilling to enter the palace, ask yourself this question: "What holds me back?" What keeps me from knowing and loving and being loved by God in the very depth of my soul? Am I still wandering around the palace because I am afraid of being close to the King? Am I just too distracted to even look for the entrance? The Psalms are full of believers running into the presence of the King seeking His face and His ways. Maybe we are afraid we don't belong. Maybe we are having enough fun without the King as He sits and waits for us to come and be with Him. He is a jealous God who longs for our love. Where are we spending our love: lavishly on Him, or are we chasing after the world's commodities?

Read Psalm 24:1-5; Psalm 51:1-7

5. Who may ascend the hill of the Lord? Who can stand in the holy place? Who does this Psalm say God is?

How can we possibly approach God? Do we have "clean hands and a pure heart?" On my best days I am soiled and on my worst days I have been living in a pig pen. I'm not talking about my house, because it is very clean! But my heart, oh, that is a far different matter. I can be filled with resentment and anger and feelings of revenge and that is all just while making my family lunch! I am so much like Cinderella and instead of dancing with the Prince of Peace I am in a heap of all kinds of emotions. My heart is often not ready for the palace because I am busy sweeping the ashes of yesterdays sorrows or today's disappointments. Do you ever live like this? I wish and pray for God to "do something;" His mercies are new every morning, but I find I am not awake in the morning, my heart is asleep. My spirit is not "awake" to the ways of God, and I am lulled to sleep by a loud and demanding world which distracts me from God and His house. "Wake up!" and ascend the hill of the Lord.

The call is to go to the house of God, to go to God Himself, but to get there I often have to remind my heart of all Christ has done for me. Emotions aside, I do not have clean hands or a pure heart, but God is able to wash me whiter than snow so that I might be close to Him. I need to be attuned to the character of God and let the picture of His holiness and greatness wake me and fill me. While the ancient gates prepare for the entrance of the King of glory, do we prepare for His entrance? Do we swing wide the gates of our hearts and allow God to come in? He longs to be lifted up, but He also longs to dwell with us. "The Lord is close to the broken-hearted and saves those who are crushed in spirit" (Psalm 34:18). Allow God to be close to you, allow Him to bind up your hurts and let Him hold you. Psalm 73:23 says, "Yet I am always with You; You hold me by my right hand. You guide me with Your counsel, and afterward You will take me into glory. Whom have I in heaven but You? And earth has nothing I desire besides You. My flesh and my heart may fail, but God is the strength of my heart and my portion forever...But as for me, it is good to be near God. I have made the Sovereign Lord my refuge; I will tell of all Your deeds." Have I made the Sovereign Lord my refuge? Do I consider it "good" to be near God? Those are some thoughts to ponder.

Read Psalm 16:1, 2; 1 John 2:28-1 John 3:3

6. Do I long for God? What does God call us in 1 John?

God extends a lavish love to us in these verses. God simply wants us to be His dearly loved children. He wants us to continue on "in Him," meaning continue in faith and in His ways, abiding in Him and allowing Him to lead us as children would be led. Can you do this? Is your heart free and able to trust and rest and be led like a beloved child? For so many of us this brings pain and grief. If we have had a painful childhood our whole view of being a child and approaching God is framed with pain. I wonder if you can lay the frame down and pick up the frame we find here in 1 John. This is lavish love, this is beloved-ness, this is belonging beyond compare, but it will cost you something. It will cost you broken beliefs and old ways of relating; it will cost you your identity as a victim and all the unhealthy sympathy and excuses that go with it. Honestly ask yourself which you would rather have: a comfortable, familiar broken way of being or beloved-ness and breath-taking love. Sometimes we have lived one way for so long, identified by wounds or pain or our past that we do not even know the first step to healthy identity and interactions. God does.

Listen to Augustine:

> "Beloved, now we are the sons of God;
> and it has not yet appeared what we shall
> be; we know that, when He shall appear,
> we shall be like Him; for we shall see Him
> as He is." This is a great promise; if you
> love, then follow. 'I do love," you say,
> 'but by what way am I to follow?' If the
> Lord your God has said to you, 'I am the
> truth and the life,' in desiring truth and
> longing for life, you might truly ask the
> way you could go to come to these things.
> You might say to yourself, 'A great thing
> is the truth; a great thing is the life, if only
> there were a way my soul could get them.'
> Do you ask by what way? Hear Jesus say
> at the first, 'I am the way.' Before He said
> where the way would lead, He said, 'I am
> the way.' The way where? I am the way, I
> am the truth, and I am the life.' It is not
> said to you, 'Work to find a way to come
> to the truth and life; this is not said.
> Sleepy one, arise; the way itself has come
> to you, and roused you from your sleep. If
> it has awakened you, get up and walk.
> Perhaps you are trying to walk and are not
> able, because your feet ache. How come
> your feet ache? Have you been running
> over rough places? But the Word of God
> has healed even the lame. Look, my feet

are fine, but I can't see the way. God also
has enlightened the blind. All this by
faith… when we have traveled the way and
have reached home itself, what shall be
more joyful than we?"[1]

Can you picture yourself in the words of this Early
Church Father? I want to know the way to God, and
sometimes I think I have to work hard to find the way, but
the Way comes to me! Even when I cannot walk and I
claim that my feet (or heart?) are too sore to go on,
Augustine reminds of us God's part: He is the One who
heals. God heals places in us that need healing so we may
carry on in the journey towards Home. The great lie of
our culture and our day is, "This is just the way I am."
No," a thousand times, I say, "No." This is how we may
appear, but we have not arrived yet. We have not seen
Him as He is and we shall be like Him then. Can I make
myself a little bit ready? Can I shed some of the lies and
identity that hold me from reflecting His glory here and
now? When we call our children to the dinner table we
expect them to be dressed and ready for dinner. How
much more so the Wedding Feast of the Lamb where the
bride of Christ (the Church) will come and sit with Him
and eat at that banquet. (See Revelation 19:7-9)

Allow the picture of Augustine's traveler, looking
for the way, stumbling with sore feet and blinded, to
touch your heart. Ask God where you are on the journey.
Do you have sore feet from the ways you have traveled or
the path you walked as a child or young adult? Ask Him
to heal you. Are you blind and just can't see the way?
Ask Him to make your blind eyes see. There is power in
the Name of the Lord and He would like you to come to
Him and ask for whatever it is you need to make it on this
journey Home. He wants you Home. Let Him touch all

110

the broken places so that your heart might hear His voice
of love for you, even on the path you are on right now, He
says, "I am the way, I am the truth, and I am the life"
(John 14:6). "Come to Me all you who are weary and
heavy laden, and I will give you rest" (Matthew 11:28).
Come take your place in His heart and at His table. You
are more than welcomed; God has been waiting for you
since creation began.

Read 1 Timothy 6:11-21

**7. What does Paul charge Timothy to do? What are
we to "take hold of?"**

We are called as believers, as God's children to
behave a certain way. Surely our salvation is not by
anything we do, but once Christ has given us those robes
of His, the robes that fit us for life eternal and life as a
child of the King, then we must act the part. We must
behave as God's children. We cannot dwell in His castle
if we do not "fight the good fight of the faith, if we do not
pursue righteousness, godliness, faith, love, endurance
and gentleness." As we wander in and out of the King's
chambers we find something new happening, at first we
are barely aware, but then we find it to be so: our hearts
begin to mirror our clothes. Righteousness springs up,
where there once was only revenge. Bitterness is replaced
by gentleness; meekness covers us like a cape. All we
have seen and known in the Father's room, in the King's
chambers, glows in us. He dwells in us now and we find
that His very life shines through us. We are no longer our
own, we are bought with a price, the precious blood of the
Lamb and the Father's precious love for us. Can you hear

Him calling you? Do you desire Him above all else?
Then run into His presence with gladness and joy. He is
waiting for you.

*"Father, hold us in Your strong arms when we run to
You. Keep us in Your love as we journey to You. May
our hearts find their true home in Your love. We need
You Lord."*

Chapter 9

Called to Leave a Legacy

**"Listen, O daughter, consider and give ear:
Forget your people and your father's house. The King
is enthralled with your beauty; honor Him, for He is
your Lord. The Daughter of Tyre will come with a
gift; men of wealth will seek your favor. All glorious is
the princess within her chamber; her gown is
interwoven with gold. In embroidered garments she is
led to the king; her virgin companions follow her and
are brought to you. They are led in with joy and
gladness; they enter the palace of the King. Your sons
will take the places of your fathers; you will make
them princes throughout the land" (Psalm 45:10-17).**

I have a beautiful little set of silver spoons from
my maternal grandmother. She left a legacy of a godly
life. I have her spoons, but what they represent to me is a
handful of quiet Sunday afternoons in her sitting room as
a child. I treasured the lovely, peaceful atmosphere of her
home, and I remember the desire I had as a small girl to
"grow up and live like Grandma." For me, her legacy had
tremendous influence, because I grew up in an
atmosphere of chaos and alcoholism. How my
grandmother chose to live her life left me a legacy I could
hold onto. As we consider our princess now in the
presence of the king we need to ask ourselves a few
questions. What difference will it make in my life and on
the legacy I leave if I spend time with the King? How

will my life be different and how will my sons' lives and my daughter's life be different because I have spent time with the King? Am I living a life that makes a godly impact on my children?

Read 2 Chronicles 34:1-8, 29-33

1. What did Josiah do when the Book of the Law was found? What kind of action did he take? What kind of legacy did he leave in Israel?

When we consider what condition Israel was in when Josiah became King, it is staggering to consider what he did. Have you ever felt that the circumstances you were in were too overwhelming to change? How about being a twelve year old and finding a Book of Laws that your fathers didn't keep? Josiah's first response is mourning. When our fathers have not kept God's ways then mourning must be a part of our lives; if I have not gotten a true picture of godliness and love as a child, then my heart surely has been wounded, if only in the way of not understanding unconditional love. I'm not saying any parent can be perfect, but I am saying that evil and its effects have repercussions in our lives. Take time to mourn them. Tear your clothes and grieve all that you did not know could not have understood as a child and then get up and inquire of the Lord. Never allow what has happened to you as a child or at any time to dictate the kind of legacy you will leave. Josiah decided he cared more about what God wanted than how he felt or what he missed or how his experiences affected him. He had a boldness and courage that I sometimes lack. He went after every kind of idolatry he found in Israel. I want to be like that; I want to look in my heart and life and find the "high places" where I am still worshiping and raising asherah poles. I know what mine are, do you? I still worship at the altar of, "do you like me?" I still burn incense to false gods when I ask myself if I fit in, or if I'm good enough. I can't know your wounds, but remember John Chrysostom's words, to "know your wounds, that you might apply the medicines."[1]

Chrysostom also writes,

> "See, we have been shown five ways of repentance: first, condemning our own sins (awake your conscience, that inward accuser), next the forgiveness of our neighbor's sins, thirdly, prayer, fourth almsgiving (compassion on the poor), fifth, humility. Do not be lazy, but walk in all these day by day... Having learned then the healing of your wounds, let us constantly apply these medicines in order that we may return to health."[2]

When we ask the Healer of our hearts to heal our wounds, we will find that the false gods and the "high places" where we make sacrifices to the wrong things will be torn down. Our wounds send us running to the high places in our lives so that we might worship the false gods we have found had along the way, whatever they might be: security, success, popularity, power, and people – pleasing. Our "medicines," according to Chrysostom, send us straight to the heart of God to deal with our wounds there. When we are humble we break down the high place of pride. When we condemn our own sins, we focus on our own wrong attitudes and not on others'. When we forgive others' wrongs we break down the high place of wounded-ness. We can ask the Healer of our hearts to come and meet us. When we apply Chrysostom's medicines, we will find freedom and joy as we live from humility and confession, from giving thanks and showing mercy. My healing depends on whether or not I am willing to, "Apply the medicines". Chrysostom even warns us not to become lazy, but to walk in these virtues day by day. When I am daily confessing my own sin, forgiving others, praying, giving to the poor and walking in humility the Lord is able to bring me health and healing. Prayer and forgiveness, repentance, humility and giving are the ways that God's people live and move and have their being. When we are living out of fear or insecurity or anger or greed, we are worshipping at the "high places." Ask yourself, "Where do I live from? Do I live from a wound that always leaves me far from God and His medicines or do I live from a place of abundant life, where all I need is found in the heart of My Father?" We leave a legacy either way. We can leave a legacy of pain or possibility, of poor choices or the God who says to us, "Behold, I am doing a new thing" (Isaiah 43:19). Ask yourself where you are living from and what kind of legacy that life will leave behind. My Grandmother, in her simple way, lived for the Lord. I remembered that legacy long after I left my chaotic childhood. What legacy am I leaving?

Read Psalm 78:1-7

2. What does the Psalmist say to share with the next generation? Why do we teach our children?

Sometimes I get things all mixed up as far as my children are concerned. I think that I need to provide everything for them, that I need to "make sure" they are walking with God and learning all they can about their faith. Some of what I believe is accurate, but some is not; I am called to tell the next generation the "praiseworthy deeds of the Lord, his power and the wonders He has done" (Psalm 78:4). I am called to tell the next generation all I know of God's power and love. I am not required to make sure they walk with Him. I would like to believe they will, but I am not responsible for my children's walk with God or obedience to Him. I am responsible, however, for having an experience of God myself. I need to have a story to share, a hope to give. "But in your hearts set apart Christ as Lord. Always be prepared to give an answer to everyone who asks you to give a reason for the hope that you have. Do this with gentleness and respect" (1 Peter 3:15). I can tell my children what I know of God. The Psalmist doesn't tell us that these children wanted to hear of God's praiseworthy deeds, but they would hear.

History requires that we tell the next generation who God is because He will be known. Either we can lead our children towards God (as Josiah did) or we can lead our children away from God (as the forefathers of the Israelites did), there is no "middle ground" here. We are either bringing God glory by the way we are living and worshiping or we are not. How about you? Are you leaving a legacy of love and forgiveness for the next generation? We will not be perfect, but God will ask us if we loved Him and others in His Name. We can choose to share all we know of God and His ways with the next generation, or we can remain silent and busy. I don't want my legacy to my children to be, "she shopped well." My mother's legacy to me still has impact on the next generation: I have her pie recipes and some of her ability to sew. I won't carry on the alcoholic, dependent and chaotic life though; my children don't need that legacy. I choose to be ruthless with the legacy I leave. I am a bit like Josiah, cutting asherah poles and grinding the dust of all that chaos and spreading it over my ancestor's graves. A gruesome picture, but I choose to leave a certain kind of legacy, and I choose to "cut off" parts of the legacy I have received so that my children do not suffer that way. Alcoholism and chaos aren't the only legacies that need to be cut off. Does anything need to be "cut up and cut off" in your family history. Are there any ways of relating, ways of loving which need to be turned over to God?

Read Psalm 78:35-43; 52-55

3. What did God do for His people in Psalm 78?

God remains faithful to us even when we are unfaithful. 2 Timothy 2:11-13 tells us, "If we died with Him, we will also live with Him; if we endure, we will also reign with Him; If we disown Him, He will also disown us; if we are faithless, He will remain faithful, for He cannot disown Himself." God redeems and rescues and helps the Israelites over and over again in this Psalm. He forgives, He is merciful, He guides them safely, He chooses and loves them. When I live my life aware of God's presence and help I can more readily share this hope and divine help with my children. You see, whether we like it or not, the legacy we leave is our life. What have we built with others? What we have built in our lives with will be all that is left to our children. I have wonderful sewing notions- zippers, buttons and lace of my Mom's, but I have no sense of how to walk with God from her; I can only sit at God's feet and ask Him to show me the way.

In the New Testament there is a picture of building materials: "If any man would build on this foundation using gold, silver, costly stones, wood hay or straw, his work will be shown for what it is, because the Day will bring it to light. It will be revealed with fire and the fire will test the quality of each man's work" (1 Corinthians 3:12, 13). I need to listen to God's words when I choose my building materials. Am I using faith, hope, and love, or fear, insecurity and mistrust? What I build my life and my family's life with is the legacy I leave for my children and the next generation. I can pick up scraps of old patterns and ways of relating, or I can ask God how to love and live in His ways. The pull is so strong in me towards mistrust and fear that I do not even realize I am living at that "high place," but I am. My family knows it because I begin to live in ways that do not honor God. The whole of Israel's laws were given to show God's people how to live God's way. When I am living God's way I find that love and faithfulness, freedom and joy are part of my daily experiences. When I am living at the "high places" of false gods my life is in ruins. I am filled with all kinds of false expectations, demands and requirements of others that do not reflect God or His ways. It takes diligence to keep our hearts free from false gods and idol worship. If I am to leave a godly legacy for my family, I will need to keep my heart loyal to God and His ways.

Read Psalm 107:1-9; 20, 21

4. How many times in this Psalm do the Israelites "cry out to God?"

Over and over again the Israelites cry out to God and He hears them; He cares for them and He forgives them. I find verse 20 fascinating: "He sent forth His word and healed them; He saved them from their distress." God longs to use His word in my life in a way that brings hope and healing. If I am storing up treasures to give my children- an inheritance of sorts, are God's hope and healing among them? In my "little girl's heart," my Grandmother's house was like a seed of hope planted in my heart. Long before I saw any way out of the home I grew up in, God showed me a picture of what life could look like: I could have tea in a quiet room visiting with others. There could be order and kindness and comfort. If I take this picture and apply it to my spiritual life the message goes so much deeper: I can cry out to God and ask for His help. On a daily basis I can run to Him and be led into His chambers with joy. I can live a life where He leads me and comforts me and knows me. I do not have to run from pain, only run to Him. He longs to walk with me and journey with me and teach my children. He longs to raise my sons up as "princes in the land," but only as I leave them in His hands.

As we read this "history lesson" in Psalm 107 we realize that the Israelites were just like us, and just like them, the key to leaving a legacy is crying out to God and giving Him thanks. Giving God thanks unlocks the heart of the next generation. We cannot control what they believe, but we can plant the seeds of faith and water their hearts with the praise of God. "Let them give thanks to the Lord for His unfailing love and His wonderful deeds for men" (Psalm 107:8, 15, 21, 31).

Read Psalm 107:10-22

5. What does God do for His people?

God chooses to gather us, lead us, satisfy us, fill us, discipline us, bring us out of darkness, save us, and break the chains that hold us, heal us, rescue us, calm the waters around us, bless us and lift us out of our affliction. What are we missing? What part of God's provision and care and love have we not recognized? If I could live my life in awareness that every breath I breathe is a gift from God, "that He gives us all things for our enjoyment" (1 Timothy 6:17), then my life would be a living legacy to all that God has done for me. Has God gathered you to Himself? Have you praised Him for that to your children? Has God led you and guided you? Take every one of those ways God helped the Israelites and if He has helped you in the same way, begin by praising Him and blessing His name to your children. Let us be sure to "tell of His works with songs of joy." Live your life in such a way that when you are with the next generation they wonder about the source of your joy and hope.

We cannot ask the next generation to praise Him and follow Him when they have not seen joy and love and mercy flow from our own hearts. May we be so filled in the Lord's presence that when we leave we have the "face of Moses;" that our hearts and lives just glow with the glory of God. If we cannot live this way, changed and healed by God's word, then how do we expect the next generation to long for God. Our grief over past sin and our healing by God's word opens the door for our heart to be a mirror of God's love. Clean the mirror of your heart. Remove the idols, the places where you are looking for love and approval that do not bring God glory- tear down all of your high places and come before God asking for Him to heal you. He loves you -- let it sink into your very being, so that you might live out of that love for the next generation.

Read Psalm 90:1, 2; 12-17

6. Who or what is our dwelling place? Who establishes the work of our hands?

Our culture is filled with people who want to be established or get established. A doctor goes to school for years and years and then he wants to get "established" in his practice. Our children grow up and go off to college and we want them to "get established." God's word in the

Psalms is filled with this picture of righteous people being "established like a tree". "The righteous will flourish like a palm tree" (Psalm 92:12-15). "I am like an olive tree flourishing in the courts of God" (Psalm 52:8), and the righteous man of Psalm 1 is, "Like a tree planted by streams of water, which yields its fruit in season and whose leaf does not wither. Whatever he does prospers." The picture should not be lost on us. What tree do you know that lasts only one generation? I am convinced that a life well-lived for God will be a legacy for the next generation, no matter when that person decides to stop living for self and surrender to God. If I declare to God that I am willing to leave the idolatry of my culture behind and "burn the asherah poles and grind the dust on the graves of common people," perhaps God can use me. If I will "tear my clothes" when I hear God's word, God will know that His word has an impact on my heart and that change in me may touch the lives of the next generation. But if I remain unmoved by God's word and His ways in my life, if I am unaware of His power and His presence, then I hold God in contempt, because He is at work and He is powerful -- I just do not have the spiritual eyes to see it or the time to notice.

May I never be so busy that I cannot see God and His ways. May my heart be broken by my sin and not so filled with criticism of those who don't act as I think they should. Can God use me to reach the next generation? The question can be answered when I consider this: where is my dwelling place? If my dwelling place is the Lord Almighty, then I can love and extend grace and mercy from the heart of God, but if I am on a hilltop worshiping the gods of self and ease, then I have some work to do. Leaving false gods behind is a very difficult task. If we have lived all our lives in the wake of self and fear, shame and pride, or whatever the sin that holds you, then we have to destroy those man-made self-imposed idols and be free to serve God. In the New Testament Jude encourages us with these words: "To those who have been called, who are loved by the God the Father, and kept by Jesus Christ: mercy and peace and love be yours in abundance. My dear friends, although I was eager to write you about the salvation we share, I felt I had to write to urge you to contend for the faith that was once entrusted to all the saints" (verses 1-3). We have been given a huge trust, and yet, if we are busy tending the fires of our own idolatry we will not be available to God "to contend for our faith." Yes, our lives are difficult at times, but when we learn to cry out to God and trust Him to care for us, and when we pray, "God, establish the work of our hands, yes, establish the work of our hands" (Psalm 90:17), God can give us a heart of wisdom. When we have learned to number our days praying, "God, this is the life You have given me, I don't know for how long, help me to walk with You in this day," then our hearts become aware of God and His faithfulness and our life becomes a legacy for Him.

Read Psalm 112:1-8

7. Can we really pray, if we have children, that God will make our children "mighty in the land?"

This is bold. The Psalmist at the beginning of our study asks God to make princes of our sons and now this

Psalmist asks God to make his children mighty in the land. I pray this. Perhaps I am naïve and take God's word too literally, but I pray for God to make our children mighty in the land. I want them to have impact and affect the next generation after them. I want them to stand up in our culture, to stand for righteousness and truth, for God and Who He is. I long for our sons and daughter to grow up and let God use them in mighty ways. I don't know what all that looks like, but I know it begins in my own heart and life. If I can cleanse my own life from idols and false beliefs then God can begin to impart truth to my children through me. He can use me or His word or anything else He chooses, but I know He tells me it is part of my job-description: tell your children of My awesome deeds and what I have done for you. Do I have anything to tell them? Do I have a legacy to leave?

"God, would You break our hearts and help us to mourn the sin in our lives? Enable us to share who You are with our children. Give us hearts that know You and lives that share You. Amen."

Chapter 10

Called to Impact the Generations

"Listen, O daughter, consider and give ear: Forget your people and your father's house. The King is enthralled by your beauty; honor Him, for He is your Lord. The Daughter of Tyre will come with a gift; men of wealth will seek your favor. All glorious is the princess in her chamber; her gown is interwoven with gold. In embroidered garments she is led to the King; her virgin companions follow her and are brought to you. They are led in with joy and gladness; they enter the palace of the King. Your sons will take the place of your fathers; you will make them princes in the land. I will perpetuate your memory through all generations; therefore the nations will praise you for ever and ever" (Psalm 45:10-17).

Here we have our princess dressed in fine garments, in the king's palace, investing in the next generation and now praising the King's Name. If we will consider that we are the bride of Christ and that He has called us to forget our people and our father's house, that He has dressed us in garments of salvation and has called us into His dwelling place, we will realize that as we are there in His presence, we can do nothing but praise His holy Name. Surely we will bring companions with us on our journey to the King, for we would want none to miss the opportunity of knowing Him; but as we are there in the presence of the King, we will find ourselves worshipping, loving and giving ourselves to the King. If we are to impact the generations then we will need to be in the King's presence, changed by His love.

Read Psalm 15:1-5

1. How readily do you approach God?

As a little girl we had a mulberry tree in our front yard, and as children, we would play baseball in bare feet under the mulberry tree. If you know anything about mulberries, it is that the berries are a bright purple and after several times around the bases, one was sure to have stained feet. I remember as a child scrubbing and scrubbing, as hard as I could to get the stains out; they never did come out…they only faded to a less visible intensity. What a picture that is for me of the evil and sin I grew up with. I remember my pastor assuring me that God could make me clean, but that pastor didn't really know how deep the stains of sin went, how many generations of sin, how many offenses, how deep the "mulberry stains" had gone.

Sin is sin and the stain of sin affects us all, but I somehow felt that nothing I could do would make me worthy to be in God's presence. Of course, I was right. Nothing *I* could do could make me righteous in the sight of God--only through what Christ has done am I made righteous. It took years and years for the effects of the "stain" of sin to fade from my heart. I felt its presence, I worried it hadn't "faded" enough. In reality I was clean because I had accepted Christ's work on the cross. How about you? Do you know that you have clean hands and a pure heart because they are gifts from God? Each day as I guard this gift of righteousness and the precious gifts of mercy and grace, I find that I am nearer to God in my humble admission of sin, and that He cleanses me. 1 John 1:9 says, "If we confess our sins He is faithful and just to forgive us our sins and cleanse us from all unrighteousness." I could be cleansed; I just had to trust the One who washed me. Can you say you will ascend the hill of the Lord because He has given you a pure heart and clean hands? All your days you can know that He has washed you whiter than snow-- even if you played in the mulberries as a child.

Read Hebrews 12:1-7; 1 Peter 1:3-7

2. Why are we called to endure hardships and suffering and discipline?

Holiness is the trademark of the Christian. If we are to be in God's presence and walk in His ways, then we are to be holy. There is no other way to have God known in our lives. Hebrews 12:14 says, "Make every effort to live in peace with all men and to be holy; without holiness no one will see the Lord." I want to make an impact on the next generation, and the way to do that is to be holy. I can show Christ to the world when I walk in holiness and obedience. I can change the world by loving. How about you? Are you walking in holiness, are you living in a way that others will see the Lord because of your life? Others will know I am God's own child when I act like it. I have to make sure that my heart is awash in the grace of God. "See to it that no one misses the grace of God and that no bitter root grows up to cause trouble and defile many" (Hebrews 12:15).

Grace is my stronghold, grace is my anchor. I can rest my soul in the grace of God because I know His grace abounds to me. Grace, says Webster's Dictionary, is "to confer dignity and honor upon, to adorn or embellish." God takes a little girl stained with mulberries and sins of her own and others, and He gives her dignity. The fairytale is as simple as that. Hans Christian Anderson says, "Every man's life is a fairytale written by the hand of God." Is this true of me or you? Could I be so open to God's grace and truth in my life that I could be a reflection of His holiness? God longs to dress me in Christ's robes of righteousness and His garments of salvation. Am I willing to give up my sin and all the sin that so easily entangles me so that I might be ready to be adorned by Him and His love? God would want me to get rid of bitterness, anger, rage, slander, envy, jealousy, or an unforgiving spirit. Are any of these lingering? If I do not "take off" these attitudes and purify my heart and mind, then I will not be able to be "clothed with Christ" or to be holy and so reveal Christ to the world. No, we will not be perfect, but each time we slander or judge another, we take a little of Christ off and put more of our "old self" on. What do I want to wear? What do you want to wear? What will impact the next generation?

Read John 15:1-6; 9, 11

3. What does the God need to prune in you?

    We have a beautiful patch of woods near our home, but it is filled with an invasive vine. In the summer one can hardly tell what part of the woods is poisonous or what part is the healthy tree. Come autumn, though, when the leaves fall and the conditions worsen, the invasive vine is easily recognizable. I used to look at the strength of the invasive vine and worry if the tree would ever live again--its branches had been bent by the weight of vines choking off the life of it. But one day I just started cutting the vine at the root and watched, amazed, as the tree began to grow upright and towards the sun.

    Sin is like that. I can give it all kinds of power in my life; past hurts and wounds and words spoken or unspoken can hold me, almost paralyzed in my growth as I "wish" that circumstances or words or conversations had gone differently. I have always puzzled over the verses in the Old Testament about God "visiting the sins of the fathers on the second and third generations" (Exodus 20:5, 6), but one must keep reading! God shows His love to "a thousand generations of those who love Him and keep His commands." God's grace pours out over the generations, thousands of them, when we are abiding in Him and choosing His ways over any past sin or someone else's past sin. The reality of God's grace in our lives is more clearly spoken in John 15. God is a gardener, and He will cut off whatever is in us that does not bear fruit. It is finished. The end. There is no more power to sin

other than our willingness and propensity to remain in it.
Jesus says, "Remain in me." "Abide in Me." "Obey My
commandments." These are words of choosing. We
choose sin--even the subtle sins of heart and attitude
towards those who are not who we want them to be or are
not acting the way we want them to act. We must choose
love. We must choose to live in God's grace and extend
that even to the "unlovable."

Can our hearts dare to give honor, dignity, adorn
or embellish another with all the love and kindness our
hearts so desperately desire? Can I give the gift of grace,
honor and dignity even to those I do not respect and do
not "like", or who do not love me the way I need them
to? These are very hard questions, but as we think about
impacting the next generations, will it be with love? If we
can love well, we have lived the greatest commandment,
and to love well, I am learning, is to love when I am
sorely disappointed, when I am keenly hurt, even when I
am wounded.

Augustine says this,

> "So is this world to all the faithful seeking
> their own country, as was the desert to the
> people of Israel? They wandered indeed as
> yet, and were seeking their own country:
> but with God for their guide they could not
> wander astray. Their way was God's
> bidding. For where they went about during
> forty years, the journey itself is made up of
> very few stations, and is known to all.
> They were retarded because they were in
> training, not because they were forsaken.
> That therefore which God promises us is

ineffable sweetness and a good as scripture
says, and as you have often heard from us
rehearsed, 'eye has not seen , nor ear
heard, nor has it entered into the heart of
man'. But by temporal labors are we
exercised, and by temptations of this
present life are we trained. If you would
not die of thirst in this wilderness, drink
charity. (Charity being defined as holding
someone dear or treasured.) It is the
fountain which God has been pleased to
place here that we will not faint on the
way: and we shall more abundantly drink
when we come into our own land. We
have made an agreement in prayer with our
God, that if we would desire that He would
forgive us our sins, we also should forgive
the sins which may have been committed
against us. Now what forgives in us is
charity. Take away charity from the heart;
hatred possesses, it knows not how to
forgive. Let charity be there, and she
fearlessly forgives. It is by charity that
other things come to be rightly loved; then
how must it be loved! Don't let charity,
which never ought to depart from the heart,
depart from the tongue." [1]

What we have learned here is that our hearts must
be wrapped in charity. Our eyes and our hearts must look
upon our world and allow grace to be the lens. We must
be willing to see others as Jesus would see them, to see
our fellow sinners as Jesus sees them, to talk to our loved
ones as Jesus would. Can we hold others "dear and

treasured?" There is no place in our lives for petty hurts and wounds that hold us and keep us from loving.

Read 1 Corinthians 13:4-8b.

4. How do you love?

What kind of love is this? Can I show this love to others on my "best days?" How about my worst days, when I'm tired and wounded and worn out? Can I love in a way that my husband, my children and my friends and the next generation know that I am God's child? I cannot win others with pious words and a wounded heart. My love must spring from a well deeper than that. I must love as Jesus loves me. I disappoint Him, He loves me. I fail Him, He loves me. I forget Him and neglect our relationship, He still loves me. "Nothing can separate me from the love of God which is in Christ Jesus Our Lord" (Romans 8:29). Yet, I separate myself and call it "good boundaries" and then, too, call it "keeping a safe distance". Loving as Jesus loves is not safe. Will I choose to abide in Christ in such a way that I can love as He loves?

Read Matthew 7:16-20; Colossians 1:10; and Philippians 1:9-11

5. What kind of tree do you want to be?

Our life can be like "a tree planted by streams of water that yields its fruit in season" (Psalm 1:3), or our life can be a tree that is weighed down by sin that has not been cut off and removed from our lives. If we want to live a life like a tree that is planted near streams of living water, then we need to be close to God. It sounds so simple, but do we approach each day, each relationship and each moment and ask God, "How can I love like You today? How can your holiness be seen in my life? How can you be seen in my life?" Allow God access to your heart and you may be surprised at all that lurks there. Do we have a heart that seeks Him and His ways, or do we selfishly want our own ways? "For My thoughts are not your thoughts and My ways are not your ways, declares the Lord" (Isaiah 55:8).

If I am serious about living for God, it will make me uncomfortable. I will need to ask God for charity to fill my heart for those I think I cannot forgive or cannot love or that I do not want to be close to. I will need to lay down my ideas about how to love in this world and ask God who He wants me to love and how He wants me to love them. It may mean letting go, it may mean forgiving a despicable person. It always means loving deeply, for "Love covers a multitude of sins" (1 Peter 4:8). I will have to ask God for that love. We have been given a great treasure -- Christ living in us -- but we have to make room for Him to live there. If I am so full of myself and how I think things and people "should" look in my life, then perhaps there is "no room" for Jesus in me. Is there room for Jesus in you? I don't mean in a Christmas carol kind of way. I mean in a painful, heart-wrenching, "God, how can I love this person" kind of way. Ask God if there is room in your heart for Him to not only dwell, but reign there. He wants to be known in the world, and the way He is known is if our lives and our hearts and our mouths proclaim Him. I want my life to be a place where people can "pick" the fruit of God; a place where they can find joy and acceptance, kindness and grace. I've got a long way to go, but as I dwell closer and closer to God, I find I am learning to see others as He would see them.

Read Ezekiel 28:25-28; Isaiah 42:6-11

6. In the history lesson for the Israelites what was important to God about His holiness?

God will show Himself to be holy among us; He will not share His glory. We are His chosen people as Israel was, and we are called to be holy. He has called us in righteousness, and the same power that raised Jesus from the dead is alive and active in us. What part of our heart or mind doesn't believe that we can be holy? We live in a sin-saturated culture, with so many running the bases with "mulberry stains." But God calls us to be set apart to Him and to have His glory displayed in our lives. When we declare the praises of the Lord and show His righteousness in our lives, even when "our lives" don't appear to be going as well as we would like, then we can begin to live as Job, "Though He slay me, yet will I trust in Him" (Job 13:15). We can stand and cling and abide, and rest in the love God has for us. We can let this world go and remind ourselves that we are not here to be "made happy," we are here to reflect our King's glory. Is His holiness being shown among us? Have we let go of idols and all that we hold as dearer than our Lord? God has called us to be a light, to free prisoners, to bring those who sit in darkness into His marvelous light. Can we do this if we are still sitting in our own darkness with the chains of our own sins and attitudes, judgments and wounds? Let all that go--all that you hold onto so tightly--and take your Savior's Hand. He longs to lead you. He calls you in grace to walk in His glory. Are you ready or willing?

Read Psalm 84: 1-5, 7-10; Matthew 10:29-31.

7. Where have you built your nest, and whose are you?

We have a little bird's nest sitting in a tiny bush next to our driveway. Each day I drive in and out several times and I am reminded: I'm building a nest. Yes, I have a family and need to shelter them, but also, my whole life is really a nest. It is a place I can find and give rest and shelter and comfort. I can find pleasures there and the company of family and good friends. All that I choose to build my nest with expresses what is in my heart. I can build with love and gentleness and mercy. I can choose hope and joy and forgiveness. I can wrap my loved ones with freedom and grace as their shelter. God reminds me so carefully in the Psalms that the sparrow found a home and the swallow a nest near God. Maybe some of you already have grown children or you don't have children at all, but even so, you have a nest--a place near the altar of God if you choose.

All your life is an unbroken song--a longing in your heart to be nearer to God. Every move, every friend, every child, every hurt has the possibility of bringing you to Your Father's heart, to your Father's Home, to Your God's altar, to be held by Him, loved by Him, known by Him. Allow the King of Kings and the Lord of Lord's to love you this way. I pray that your heart might hear Him calling you by His grace to live in His glory. I pray that you might build your nest so close to the altar of God that your heart is able to hear His songs of love for you: "The Lord your God is with you, He is mighty to save. He will take great delight in you, He will quiet you with His love, He will rejoice over you with singing" (Zephaniah 3:17).

In closing, listen to the words of Augustine:

> "The sparrow has found herself a home;
> my heart has found itself a home. She tries
> her wings at the virtues of this life, in faith,
> and hope and love, by which she may fly
> to her home...A home is chosen forever, a
> nest is framed for a time...with the heart
> we think upon God, as if the sparrow flew
> to her home; with the flesh (our body here)
> we do good works: break your bread for
> the hungry, bring the poor and roofless into
> your house and if you see one naked,
> clothe him."[2]

I realize my heart has found a home and I am free to build a lovely little nest. I can frame a nest worthy of God's glory and know my heart has a home in Him. So, fly home, dear child of God. Know that you also have a home and you are on your way to a Father of infinite grace and love. Frame your nest well; love and live with all your heart open and ready to give to the world all He has given you. Know that you are called by grace to live for His glory.

"To Him who is able to keep you from falling and present you before His glorious presence without fault and with great joy--to the only God our savior be glory and majesty, power and authority, through Jesus Christ our Lord, before all ages, now and forever more" (Jude 24-25).

NOTES

Chapter 1
1. John Chrysostom, Letters to Olympias I.1; NPNF1 9:289.
2. John Chrysostom, Selected Homilies II.5; NPNF1 9:189.
Chapter 2
1. Augustine, Sermons on the New Testament Lessons LXXXIV.2; NPNF1 6:510.
Chapter 3
1. John Chrysostom, Homilies on St. John II.11; NPNF1 4:9.
2. John Chrysostom, Two Homilies on Eutropius II.15; NPNF1 9:263.
Chapter 4
1. John Chrysostom, The Gospel of Matthew Homily XXXI.2; NPNF1 10:207.
Chapter 5
1. John Chrysostom, Two Homilies on Eutropius II.14; NPNF1 9:262.
Chapter 6
1. John Chrysostom, Letters to the Fallen Theodore I.2; NPNF1 9:92.
Chapter 7
1. Augustine, Psalm LXXXV.6; NPNF1 8:406.
Chapter 8
1. Augustine, On the Gospel of John XXXIV.9; NPNF1 7:203.
Chapter 9
1. John Chrysostom, Augustine Against Those who say that Demons Govern Human Affairs Homily II.5; NPNF1 9:189.
2. John Chrysostom, Against Those who say that Demons Govern Human Affairs Homily Homily II.6 NPNF1 9:190.
Chapter 10
1. Augustine, Homily VII.1; NPNF1 7:501-502.
2. Augustine, Psalm LXXXIV.7; NPNF1 8:401.

Abbreviations: NPNF1 = Nicene and Post-Nicene Fathers, First Series, Hendrickson Publishers